The Friendly Invasion of
Leominster

The Friendly Invasion of
Leominster

An account of the U.S. Military units billeted around Leominster, Herefordshire, 1943-1945

Fran & Martin Collins

BREWIN BOOKS

First published by
Brewin Books Ltd, 19 Enfield Ind. Estate,
Redditch, Worcestershire, B97 6BY in 2012
www.brewinbooks.com

Reprinted September 2020

© Fran & Martin Collins 2012
All rights reserved

ISBN: 978-1-85858-493-5

The moral rights of the authors have been asserted

A Cataloguing in Publication Record
for this title is available from the British Library

Typeset in Adobe Garamond
Printed in Great Britain by 4edge Ltd

CONTENTS

Introduction	Leominster: Raided and Invaded	vi
Chapter 1	Tough Ombres at Berrington Hall	1
Chapter 2	Rangers Lead the Way	24
Chapter 3	The Lucky Seventh	33
Chapter 4	A Diamond in the Rough (76th General Hospital)	43
Chapter 5	A Job Well Done (76th General Hospital)	54
Chapter 6	The Battle of General Mud (76th General Hospital)	62
Chapter 7	Bridging the Gap Between the Hospital Bed and the Foxhole (135th General Hospital)	82
Chapter 8	Medically Approved Individual and Group Recreation (135th General Hospital)	91
Chapter 9	Two Allied Friendly Nations (135th General Hospital)	104
Chapter 10	A Fragment of History	114
Appendix 1	Abbreviations	124
Appendix 2	Glossary	126
Appendix 3	American Units Based in Leominster, 1944–1945	128
Appendix 4	U.S. Army Hospitals in U.K. 1944	132
	Acknowledgements	134

INTRODUCTION

LEOMINSTER: RAIDED AND INVADED

Leominster, a small market town with a population of 11,000 is situated in Herefordshire near to the Welsh border. Its recorded history goes back to the seventh century A.D. when a nunnery was founded by King Merwald of Mercia.

The town has a history of being invaded and raided. In 777A.D. Leominster's Saxon nunnery was devastated by British raiders and in 980A.D. the Danes ransacked the town. Because of its proximity to the border of Wales and its wealth due to wool production Leominster was subject to a number of raids from the Welsh. In 1052 it was raided by Guffadd ap Llywelyn and in 1207 by William de Braos of Brecknock, who burned the town to the ground. In 1402 Owain Glyndower and his army seized the town and took everything of value. During the Wars of the Roses the town's fortunes changed. Owen Tudor was captured at the nearby Battle of Mortimer's Cross and thousands of Welshmen on the losing Lancastrian side were put to the sword.

Tudor times brought mixed fortunes to Leominster. In 1539 Henry VIII seized Leominster's priory and its revenues for the crown. When Edward VI died the people of Leominster attacked the men who were behind the plot to put the Protestant Lady Jane Grey on the throne. When she came to the throne Queen Mary rewarded their loyalty by conferring a charter on the town in 1553. During the Civil War in 1643 William Waller seized Leominster for the Parliamentarians but in 1645 it was taken back by the Royalists.

INTRODUCTION – LEOMINSTER: RAIDED AND INVADED

For the next three hundred years the town enjoyed a period of comparative peace and prosperity until 1943 when it became subject to the 'friendly invasion' of Allied Forces known by the Americans by the code name: Operation Bolero.

The Priory Church of St Peter and St Paul, Leominster. Parts of the church date from 1130A.D.

CHAPTER 1

TOUGH OMBRES AT BERRINGTON HALL

The first part of Leominster to be 'invaded' by American personnel was Berrington Park (now owned by the National Trust). During the war Berrington Hall was owned by the Cawleys and, as in the First World War, the hall was used as a convalescent hospital for British troops. It was run by Lady Vivienne Cawley, who was active in the Red Cross.

The American troops did not require the use of the house, only the grounds. In 1942 farmer, William Edwards, who rented Ashton Court Farm on the Berrington estate, was informed that part of the parkland he farmed would be required by the War Department. Within a few weeks a unit of Negro Americans (the first black people he had seen) arrived to build the camp which was to be a transit camp for American troops in the build up to D-Day.

A number of Nissen huts were built in the grounds and a tented encampment was set up. The buildings included a medical centre, mess hall, P.X. and ablutions. The water supply was piped from Leominster across the Berrington parkland to high ground above North Lodge where water tanks were placed on trestles 30 feet above the ground so that the water ran by gravity to supply the huts.

It was said that Lady Cawley had ensured that crops were planted in the grounds at the front of the hall so that she would not have to look out on rows of tents. Whether this is true or not, the American encampment was situated at the back of the hall near the Triumphal Arch and west of North Lodge. In April 1943 the first unit of American soldiers arrived and were billeted in tents alongside what is now the A49 running from South Lodge to Eye Lane.

Early in 1944 a number of advance detachments for various ordnance and construction battalions arrived in Leominster. Advance detachments were composed of a small number of officers and enlisted men who would prepare suitable sites and collect equipment for the remainder of the unit prior to their arrival in England. In February 1944 advance detachments of the 66th, 312th, 314th, 316th and 317th Ordnance Battalions arrived. They were joined by advance detachments of the 33rd Signal Construction Battalion (which was to be based in Wrexham), 12th Field Artillery Observation Battalion and 96th Field Artillery Group. The 1025th Signal Company and 385th Anti Aircraft Artillery AW Battalion also arrived in Leominster in February. In April the 193rd Field Artillery Group made Leominster its temporary home.

Berrington Hall in the 1940's. Crops can be seen growing at the front of the hall (P. Edwards).

CHAPTER 1 – TOUGH OMBRES AT BERRINGTON HALL

Berrington Hall (P. Edwards).

The 359th Infantry Regiment of the 90th Infantry Division arrived at Berrington Hall on 6 April 1944. The 90th Infantry Division arrived at Liverpool between the 4th and 8th of April (An advance detachment had arrived earlier to set up some of the camps). On arrival in Liverpool the men were transported by rail to camps around the Midlands area, mainly in South East Shropshire. The Division H.Q. was set up in King Edwards Grammar School, Edgbaston, Birmingham. The 359th Regiment had left New York on 23 March aboard the *Athlone Castle*. After disembarkation in Liverpool on 5 April the men travelled by train to Berrington Park.

On arrival at the park Olavi Oja recalls the men having to put up their own tents. The men were unable to tell their family and friends where they were stationed in England but Olavi came from Fitchburg, which was close to Leominster, Massachusetts. Fitchburg and Leominster were known as sister towns so Olavi wrote to his mother that he was billeted in her town's sister town so she would be able to work out where he was.

Aerial view of Berrington Estate showing two nissen hut camps at top right hand corner (Reproduced with permission of English Heritage).

CHAPTER 1 – TOUGH OMBRES AT BERRINGTON HALL

Able Company, 33rd Signal Construction Battalion, Wrexham (Chad Phillips).

Baker Company 33rd Signal Construction Battalion (Chad Phillips).

Above: *385th Anti Aircraft AW Battalion* (Tim Eastman).

Left: *385th Anti Aircraft AW Battalion* (Tim Eastman).

Below: *Shoulder patch of the 90th Infantry Division whose nickname was Tough Ombres* (Author's collection).

CHAPTER 1 – TOUGH OMBRES AT BERRINGTON HALL

The 315th Engineers, who were attached to the 90th Division, set to work to complete some of the buildings. Details of the 315th were sent to the other camps in the Midlands like Sturt Common, Camp Gatacre and King Edwards School, where no engineer troops were stationed. When it was realised that their stay in England would not be long post engineer work was restricted to essentials.

While in England the battalion continued combat training and received and processed new equipment and supplies. On their arrival in Leominster the local people made the G.I.s feel welcome and a number invited them to their homes. Olavi remembers only going into Leominster twice, once was to church. Vernon Ellingson was invited to the homes of Mr and Mrs Harris several times. Mr Harris even wrote to Vernon's parents to let them know how Vernon was.

> "Belmont", Rylands Road
> Leominster, Hereford
> England. 8 May 1944.
>
> Dear Mrs Ellingson,
>
> It is a pleasure to have Vernon dropping in to Supper when his job permits him. He looks very well indeed and is quite happy, still keeping up his sports. Mrs Harris and I wish you too could drop in, also his girl friend. Well, while he is near enough we shall be most glad to see him whenever he is free to call. Our fields and gardens are now at their best. We send you our very kindest greetings and good wishes. Take care of yourself and you need not be at all anxious about Vernon. God bless you,
>
> B.E. Harris.

Letter written to Vernon's parents by Mr Harris (Rosanne and Joy Bliss).

Letter written by Vernon Ellingson while he was at Berrington Park (Rosanne and Joy Bliss).

Alfred Copt, a medic with the 359th, also enjoyed getting to know the local people. He remembers going for a walk in the countryside with two of his friends the day after he arrived at Berrington Park. While walking they met three girls who were rather nervous of the men at first but soon got talking and arranged to meet up at a dance in Leominster the next evening. The six were to meet up several times in the next few weeks. Another person the men of the 359th were to meet was General Patton who visited the men at Berrington Park to boost their morale before they went to France.

By 1 May the entire battalion had been fully supplied. On 13 May the 359th Regiment, Battalion Headquarters and the Medical Detachment left Leominster and travelled by train to Camp Blackbird (Station U87) twelve miles south of Abergavenny. The camp had high brick walls and the men were not allowed leave during their time there. Part of the time was spent waterproofing vehicles. They were also given small rubber containers to put billfolds and other paper items in and enough K rations for 3 days. The men were given no information about their future movements. But they were given practise in climbing cargo nets. All elements of the 90th Division were now billeted on the southern coast of Wales along the Bristol Channel.

CHAPTER 1 – TOUGH OMBRES AT BERRINGTON HALL

Vernon Ellingson (Rosanne and Joy Bliss).

Sergeant Wadie Thompson, Sergeant T. Stucke, Sergeant Charles Kell in Leominster (Olavi Oja).

Sergeant Olavi Oja and Corporal Donald Johnson at Berrington Park (Olavi Oja).

CHAPTER 1 – TOUGH OMBRES AT BERRINGTON HALL

Above left: *Corporal Johnson at Berrington Park* (Olavi Oja).

Above right: *Sergeant Olavi Oja at Berrington Park* (Olavi Oja).

Corporal Donald Johnson in the grounds of Berrington Park (Olavi Oja).

Sergeant Olavi Oja in the grounds of Berrington Park (Olavi Oja).

Sergeant Olavi Oja and Junior Fitzgerald near the Triumphal Arch in Berrington Park (Olavi Oja).

CHAPTER 1 – TOUGH OMBRES AT BERRINGTON HALL

George Winkler from the 90th Division (S. Winkler).

Morning report from Camp Blackbird (Joy and Rosanne Bliss).

U.S.S. Susan B. Anthony (U.S. Naval Historical Center).

At the end of May, at the dead of night, the men shipped out of Camp Blackbird and on the 2nd, 3rd and 4th June all elements of the 90th boarded ships at Cardiff and sailed to Bristol where they waited in the Bristol Channel for a while. The ships were on alert to sail to Normandy but because of the poor weather conditions D-Day was postponed from 5 June to 6 June and the men were kept on board an extra day. Some of the men saw a small boat visit each ship and there was speculation that final orders were being given. With hindsight it can be seen that notice of the delay of D-Day was being given. On 6 June the ships sailed around the south coast of England to join the rest of the invasion fleet in the D-Day invasion.

Medic Alfred Copt of the 359th Regiment was aboard the *U.S.S. Susan B. Anthony* with the 2nd Battalion. He remembers feeling nervous when the ship finally sailed, particularly when he was given his assault boat assignment which was number one along with 42 other infantrymen.

When the *Anthony* arrived off the coast of Normandy it was kept in reserve for the second wave of the offensive. The first wave, which included the 4th Infantry Division and elements of the 90th, was able to secure Utah Beach so there was talk of diverting the remainder of the 90th to Omaha Beach where there were heavy losses.

At around 08:00 on 7 June, before the decision could be made, the *Anthony* hit a mine which exploded under her Number 4 hold. Immediately she lost all power and her rudder went hard left and stuck. Alfred has vivid memories of that moment:

> "As we were strapping our equipment on, the ship hit a mine and was blown out of the water. I hit the ceiling and was knocked out for a while. When I woke up everyone was gone. I looked around and there was a stairway 40 or 50 feet away. Men were trapped and crying for help. A large beam had crashed through the deck above and one end was near me. I decided to climb the beam.
>
> In the darkness I could hear a soldier screaming right under me. I looked closer and saw that the beam was over his hips and he was crushed. I tried to pull it off him but could not move it. There seemed to be many soldiers crying for help. I climbed the beam."

While Alfred had been unconscious the ship had been taking on water in holds 4 and 5 and had begun to list. Commanding Officer, Commander Grey ordered the soldiers to move to the port side of the ship, thus bringing the *Anthony* back to even keel. At 08:22 the fleet tug, *Pinto*, came alongside to tow the *Anthony* to shallow water, but at this point fires erupted in the engine and fore rooms and the ship began to sink. The commander had no choice but to order 'Abandon Ship'. When the order came Alfred tried to blow up his life vest but it would not inflate. When he took it off he saw that it was torn to shreds. He noticed that a sailor had opened a large cupboard and was giving out blue cork vests, another sailor threw Alfred one and he put it on. Alfred recalls:

> "Other ships came on both sides of the sinking ship and we had to jump from one ship to the other. They ran a bunch of us right across the deck and had us jump way down to a British Destroyer. I was groggy and had a lump on my head. I went down about three steps and lay face down on someone's bed. I don't know if I lay five minutes or 20 but I woke up with a jump remembering what had just happened. I ran up a few steps and watched the Susan B. Anthony disappear to her permanent grave 500 feet down. [this was around 10:10] All I could think of was those trapped soldiers."

CHAPTER 1 – TOUGH OMBRES AT BERRINGTON HALL

Left: *Alfred Copt – medic with the 359th Regiment* (St Louis County Historical Society).

Below and bottom:
U.S.S. Susan B. Anthony (AP-72) sinking off Omaha Beach, Normandy, 7 June 1944 after striking a mine. Alongside is U.S.S. Pinto attempting to rescue survivors and fight the fires. Also in the photo is the bow ramp of L.C.T-544 coming alongside to take off survivors. Photo was taken from L.C.T-544 (U.S.S. Susan B. Anthony Reunion Organisation).

Miraculously, unbeknown to Alfred, all the crew and soldiers on the *Anthony* had been evacuated and of the 45 wounded only a small number were seriously hurt. The last member of the salvage crew jumped overboard at 10:00 closely followed by Commander Grey.

A little later assault boats came alongside the destroyers to take the 90th Division men. Alfred could see several of his 90th Division buddies in the assault boat that came alongside the destroyer he was in but they didn't recognise him as he had no helmet and was still wearing the blue life vest. Alfred was placed at the front of the assault boat. He remembers thinking about how he would be totally exposed whilst he was making his way to shore and he promptly threw up the salami sandwich he had been given while aboard the British destroyer. He recalls the landing:

> *"When we landed ... fighting was about two miles inland, but the Germans were shelling the beach with mortar and artillery. While still in knee-deep water our lieutenant was killed by shrapnel. While we were moving inland two German planes strafed us. I looked one pilot right in the face and he looked at me. They did not hit anyone."*

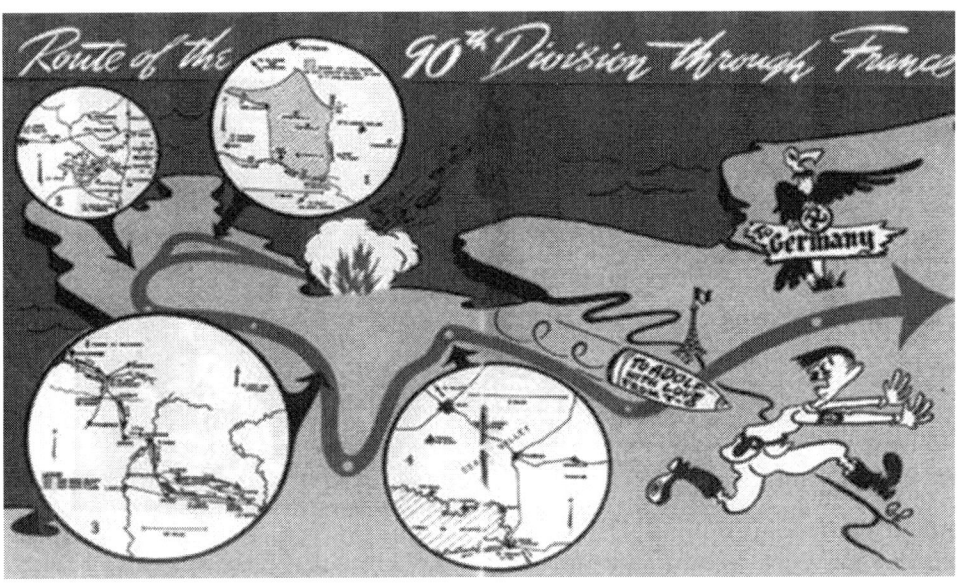

Map showing route of 90th Division through France (Tough Ombres booklet).

CHAPTER 1 – TOUGH OMBRES AT BERRINGTON HALL

Corporal Ernest Lidtke and Private Turner Shew of the 90th Division in Rezenville, France 12 October 1944 (Olavi Oja).

When Alfred reached the shore he felt useless as he had lost all his equipment aboard the *Anthony*. He was given a shovel to help dig ditches. He remembers that a man digging near him dug up a small blue plastic container. Alfred advised the man to leave it and dig elsewhere. Suddenly there was an explosion, Alfred found later that the blue container held an explosive designed for paratroopers to throw at the tracks of tanks to disable them.

Alfred was soon able to pick up a helmet and medical equipment from wounded and dead soldiers and join the rest of his regiment. From Utah Beach the division cut across Merderet and took Pont L' Abbe. In July the 90th cleared Floret de Mont-Castle known as Hill 122. Alfred was hit in the hip while helping wounded soldiers beneath Hill 122. He suffered internal bleeding and was evacuated to the 52nd General Hospital in Wolverley, Worcestershire for treatment.

T. Sergeant Joseph Steich, Gus Gennerio, Chester Horn, A. Satre and Corporal Roy Asher of the 90th Division with 'Red' the dog in the Ardennes Forest during the Battle of the Bulge. February 1945 (Olavi Oja).

Meanwhile the 90th continued to Periers. In August it crossed the Sarthe River and took part in the closing of the Falaise Gap by reaching the 1st Polish Division in Chambois. In September it crossed France via Verdun and took part in the battle for Metz, after which the division crossed the Moselle River. By December the 90th had crossed the Saar River and set up a defensive position when the Ardennes offensive began. In February the 90th breached the Siegfried Line and took Main and Werra Rivers and moved towards the Czech border. It was on route to Prague when V.E. Day was declared.

Meanwhile at the end of June 1944 the 943rd and 736th Field Artillery Battalions arrived at Berrington Park. The 736th had sailed to England on the *Queen Elizabeth*, sailing from New York on 22 June and taking the usual zig-zag course across the Atlantic. It took only seven days to reach Greenock in Scotland. The *Queen* was too large to dock so it was necessary for the men to disembark and board a smaller boat to sail down the River Clyde. It took the small boat an hour and a quarter to complete the half mile journey. Here the men got the chance to see a number of ships with battle damage, the first wreckage of war the battalion had seen. From Greenock the 736th boarded a train to Leominster.

CHAPTER 1 – TOUGH OMBRES AT BERRINGTON HALL

On 1 July the battalion received its first vehicles and on 4 July the tractors arrived. On 21 July the men were informed that the howitzers had arrived and were on a cargo ship anchored off the coast of Wales. The men took the tractors to collect the howitzers but unfortunately had difficulty towing them around the narrow lanes of Britain and at one point one of the men lost control of his tractor which ran down a hill and plunged into a brick coal shed.

Two officers from the group decided to go in the unit's Piper Cub to settle the claim with the owner of the shed. Unfortunately the take off was miscalculated and the plane ploughed into the hedge at the end of the grass landing strip. What was left of the plane was dismantled and transported away in a 2½ ton truck and the officers had to choose another method of transport to go and settle the claim.

A number of personnel from the unit were involved in accidents while collecting equipment needed for the battalion in France. On 27 July a private and corporal were involved in a collision near Kidderminster, fortunately there were no serious injuries. The next day eleven men were in a ¾ ton truck which turned over but miraculously also produced no injuries. On 29 July there was a more serious accident when a 736th vehicle taking Commander Colonel Stocks to a meeting in the south of England skidded into a 2½ ton truck on a curve. The gas tank was crushed and sprayed burning gasoline on the men. T/Sgt. Waerner was killed and two other men were badly burnt when the vehicle caught fire.

Local Leominster people remember another traffic accident in Leominster which may have involved American vehicles from the units based nearby. The accident involved the horse that pulled the parcel van. While the van was parked outside Ross's shop in the High Street a military vehicle struck the rear of the van. This caused the horse to be lifted by the shafts of the van and be propelled through the shop window onto the display shelf which collapsed, dropping the horse into the cellar. The vet had to be called to put the animal out of his misery.

On 1 August the 376th received orders to break camp and on 3 August the battalion left Berrington Park for the P.O.E. near Portsmouth. On 5 August the battalion was issued life belts, left the marshalling area and boarded the two L.S.T.s and one L.C.T. which carried the M4s, howitzers and other vehicles to France.

On arrival in France the battalion was attached to the 195th Artillery Group. It commenced travelling across France, engaging in its first battle at Querray. At the end of August the 736th crossed the River Seine and Marne. In September they were involved

Above left: *Colonel Stocks and Lt. Wildorn of the 376th on board L.S.T. in Portsmouth Harbour* (Carol and Glenn Mounts).

Above right: *Embarking on L.S.T. 2 at Portsmouth 5 August 1944* (Carol and Glenn Mounts).

Left: *736th Field Artillery Battalion crossing the Marne River 30 August 1944* (Carol and Glenn Mounts).

Below: *736th Field Artillery Battalion crossing the Seine River 27 August 1944* (Carol and Glenn Mounts).

CHAPTER 1 – TOUGH OMBRES AT BERRINGTON HALL

736th Field Artillery Battalion near Condsorf, Luxembourg (Carol and Glenn Mounts).

in the battle to take Metz but unfortunately the Germans had the upper hand as they held Fort Driant, a fortress with seven foot thick reinforced concrete walls which was on a hill on the west bank of the Moselle river. The fort also had an elaborate underground system of bunkers and observation posts. Apparently it was the best defended fort in Europe. After the loss of 500 American troops Patton decided to halt the attack.

As they moved through Europe the 736th did capture a number of Russian 12.2mm howitzers and German 88s. They found the 88s to be more accurate than the erratic Russian guns, nevertheless the authorities informed them they would have to give up the German guns.

On 15 November the battalion was finally able to cross the Moselle River and the first shots were fired into Germany by the 736th on 21 November. On 5 December Metz was finally taken, but unfortunately the German offensive made it necessary for the battalion to withdraw back into France. At the end of December the 736th moved into Luxembourg and in February 1945 it crossed the Saar River back into Germany. In March the battalion was taken off the line for the first time since arriving in France and was able to enjoy some much needed R & R. At the end of March the 736th crossed the Rhine. The last round fired by the battalion was on 3 May and on 6 May the organisation was relieved of its combat mission.

Meanwhile in November 1944 the 24th and 45th Signal Construction Battalions arrived at Leominster to prepare for moving to France.

CHAPTER 2

RANGERS LEAD THE WAY

Land on the western outskirts of Leominster was also requisitioned by the War Department for billeting American soldiers. A nissen hut camp was constructed on the land adjacent to Green Lane.

The 5th Ranger Battalion, commanded by Lieutenant Colonel Max Schneider, arrived here in January 1944. This unit had left New York on the *U.S.S. Mauretania* on 8 January 1944. Unfortunately, as the ship left the harbour, it collided with a freighter and had to be towed back for repairs. Even before the ship had completed docking scaffolding had been erected and floodlights set up to illuminate the area for overnight repairs. The following day the *Mauretania* was on its way (following the usual zig-zag course to avoid German submarines) to a 'secret destination'.

On 17 January the *Mauretania* arrived at Liverpool, England. There was a delay of 24 hours in the outer harbour because the opening through the minefield was not wide enough to allow the ship to enter the inner harbour. The help of a minesweeper was enlisted and the *Mauretania* finally docked on 18 January. The following day the Rangers travelled by train to Leominster where they were to spend the next two months preparing for D-Day. During the daytime the men trained, practising cliff scaling, rappelling (abseiling), rope bridge crossing and field exercises.

One evening, after the men had retired, one of the sergeants woke a group of men up to take part in a field exercise. The men dressed quickly and boarded a 2½ ton truck. The canvas opening was fastened across the back of the truck so that the men were in darkness and in ignorance of their surroundings. After an hour's drive the truck stopped and the Company Commander, Captain John T. Eichner, got the men out and showed the sergeant a map with no place names on, pointing to their present position. He took the map away and told them that they were in 'enemy territory' and were to find their way back to the barracks for morning assembly the following day.

When the officers and truck had departed the men of the platoon discussed any tell-tale sounds they had heard on the journey. All agreed that they had travelled over, then under two bridges and driven through a village. It was after midnight when they started out but they soon came to the village where they saw a police station. They decided to see if there was a map there they could use.

Two of the men approached the police station, which had a blackout curtain hanging in the place of a door. As the men neared the curtain it opened and two policemen came out. The Rangers fell flat on the floor to avoid being seen by the policemen whose eyes were not yet accustomed to the dark. When the policemen had gone the Rangers continued up the steps and carefully parted the curtain. From the doorway they could see a map on the wall and were able to ascertain that they needed to continue in a northerly direction. Fortunately the police sergeant behind the desk had his head bowed and didn't notice the men.

Above: *5th Rangers shoulder tab* (Author's collection).

Right: *Medics of the 5th Ranger Battalion* (Courtesy of WW2 U.S. Medical Research Center – www.med-dept.com).

The two Rangers returned to the rest of the group and by going north soon found a railway bridge to go under and a river bridge to go over. A mile further on the men found a place to sleep. After waking early the next morning the Rangers breakfasted on some cookies that some of the men had brought with them.

They started to walk and were soon able to see the hill that the two men had seen on the map in the police station. They climbed it. At the top of the hill was a church and parsonage. As the men approached the church they saw a man who started running when he saw them. Bearing in mind that they had been told that they were in enemy territory the men ran to cut him off. When they had caught up with him they found the man to be an elderly minister who was gasping for breath. He had thought they were German paratroopers.

The Rangers explained to the minister that they were on an exercise and that he would now have to play 'dead' as they had caught him. He was happy to do this and invited them to the parsonage to meet his wife. She insisted that they stay for a meal and made them sandwiches and tea. Aware of the rationing situation the Rangers gave the couple a packet of tea that one of the men had on him.

The Rangers, in combat gear and carrying weapons, made an incongruous picture sitting in the parlour of the parsonage. One of the men sat at the piano stool with his Thompson sub-machine gun lying on the floor. He couldn't resist running his fingers over the keys so the minister and his wife invited him to play. He was an accomplished pianist and entertained the group with some of the classics. Eventually, much refreshed, the men left the parsonage and arrived back at the barracks in time for roll call.

Another time, while staying in Leominster, one of the companies, which included Victor Miller, was sent to an estate in Wales to prepare billets for an engineering battalion due to arrive there. The men spent the days working and the evenings in the pub of the nearby town. The path to the pub lay across a field which was inhabited by horses and swans. One particularly large swan would chase the horses around the field and also the G.I.s when walking through the field a little worse for wear.

One night the new battalion personnel were in bed when they heard three of the Rangers shouting that they would kill someone. The three went out with bayonet, bolo and fighting knife and later returned to the camp with clothes stained with blood. The following morning the engineers discovered that their victim was the swan. The following day the Rangers returned to Leominster. This was good timing as it was found out later that it was an offence to kill birds that belonged to the crown.

Above: *Doc Felix of the Medical Detachment 5th Rangers* (Courtesy of WW2 U.S. Medical Research Center – www.med-dept.com).

Right: *Victor J. Miller* (5th Rangers).

While in Leominster the men also spent time in the pubs in the town and enjoyed making the acquaintance of local girls who thought that the Rangers were so much more glamorous then the British soldiers. The girls were also impressed at the men's arrays of medals, although the British soldiers would comment that the Americans even gave out medals for those who could spit the furthest.

At this time members of the Land Army would also spend off-duty time in the town. A number were based at Bircher Hall, four miles away. The girls from Bircher Hall would often cycle into Leominster, leave their bikes at the fire station and change into 'civvies' before going into town. One night, on their arrival at the fire station the girls were told that there was trouble in the town. They saw trucks full of M.P.s and saw fighting between black and white U.S. soldiers. The firemen advised the girls to return to their billets, which they did.

The fighting was between the Rangers and members of a black Quartermaster Truck company based just outside the town, possibly at Berrington Park. At this time the U.S. Army had a policy of segregation so black and white soldiers were unused to working or socialising together. The people of Leominster noticed that black and white American soldiers were treated differently. If a white soldier walked down a street and a black soldier was coming the other way the black soldier would step off the pavement into the road until the white soldier had passed by. In the fish and chip shops white soldiers would expect to be served before the black soldiers even if they were behind them in the queue.

Because of segregation the white soldiers felt that it was wrong for black soldiers to go out or dance with the white girls of the town and it could have been an incident of this type which started the trouble. There were a number of incidents of fighting between black and white soldiers and it has been reported that this climaxed in the stabbing of a white soldier either outside the Clifton Cinema or the fair near the station. Pauline Davies remembers a black soldier being stabbed in Etnam Street.

It became necessary for the black and white troops to be allowed into the town on separate evenings to avoid conflict. This reduced open friction but there were stories of a white unit carrying out a midnight raid on the Quartermaster unit. The Rangers denied all knowledge of this.

In March the Rangers left Leominster for Scotland where they carried out commando training and then they travelled to Swanage, Dorset, where they took part in assault and cliff training. In April their training was completed in the Fabius II landing exercise.

CHAPTER 2 – RANGERS LEAD THE WAY

Rangers training in Scotland (U.S. Military Archives).

E. Company, 5th Rangers in Landing Craft prior to landing on Omaha Beach (U.S. Military Archives).

On 6 June the 5th Rangers landed on the heavily defended Omaha Beach as part of Operation Overlord. Their mission was to support the 2nd Rangers Battalion's attack on Pointe Du Hoc. The plan was for them to land so that they could approach Pointe Du Hoc from the rear while the 2nd Rangers scaled the cliffs and attacked the German gun emplacements from the front.

The 5th were scheduled to land on the strip of beach designated 'Dog Green' but Lieutenant Colonel Schreider ordered the flotilla commander to touch down east of this position on 'Dog White' because of the heavy volume of fire.

CHAPTER 2 – RANGERS LEAD THE WAY

As the Rangers landed alongside the 29th Infantry Division, who were encountering heavy resistance, the 29th's Commander ordered that they should support the 29th before moving on to Pointe Du Hoc. At this point Assistant Division Commander, General Norman D. Cota uttered the immortal words: "Lead the way, Rangers" – a quote that was to stay with the 5th Rangers throughout the Normandy campaign.

The leading troops of the Rangers were able to climb over the sea wall, blow gaps in the barbed wire and advance to a point on top of the hill. First Lieutenant Francis W. Dawson of Company D. led his platoon over the top and eliminated an enemy strong point. The entire battalion was then able to advance towards Vierville Sur Mer, avoiding mines and clearing the area of German snipers hiding in the hedgerows, as they advanced. The unit received heavy sniper and machine gun fire. E. Company attempted to penetrate towards the south. In support C. Company knocked out several 81mm mortar concentration but they were replaced so quickly that E. Company was forced to abandon its southern attack. Heavy casualties were received.

By nightfall the battalion had advanced through Vierville Sur Mer and along with three companies of the 2nd Rangers, part of the 1st Ranger Battalion and the 743rd Tank Battalion they were able to set up perimeter defences. One platoon of Company A. which had been separated from the main part of the battalion during the crossing of the sea wall, arrived at the rallying point with twelve German prisoners.

The platoon of Company F. which landed near Laurent Sur Mer, had encountered heavy artillery and machine gun fire. It had attempted to reach Vierville Sur Mer but the men were pinned down and by nightfall had not managed to make contact with the rest of the battalion. At the end of D-Day the 5th Rangers had taken 100 prisoners and killed 150 enemy soldiers. Approximately 60 Rangers had been killed or wounded.

Over the next four days the 5th Rangers were able to enlarge and improve the beachhead and move towards Pointe Du Hoc. F. Company was able to break out of their position and move inland, taking out pillboxes and gun emplacements as it went. By the end of D+4 120 more Germans had been killed and 550 prisoners taken. There was a heavy cost to the Rangers; the unit had 114 casualties (23 K.I.A. 89 W.I.A., 2 M.I.A.). Sadly six of the casualties were to friendly fire when the tanks of the 743rd, attacking Pointe Du Hoc from the south-west, caught the Rangers in the crossfire.

Back in Leominster, shortly after D-Day the film 'Hers to Hold' was shown at the Clifton cinema. As Deanna Durbin sang 'Say a prayer for the boys over there' there were many tears and sobbing as the girls wondered what had happened to the Rangers they had got to know while they were stationed in the town.

Photo taken on D+2, after relief forces reached the Rangers at Pointe Du Hoc. The American flag had been spread out to stop fire of friendly tanks coming from inland. Some German prisoners are being moved in after capture by the relieving forces. SC190240 (U.S. Army Center for Military History).

CHAPTER 3

THE LUCKY SEVENTH

In April 1944 the advance party of the 31st Tank Battalion of the 7th Armored Division, replaced the 5th Ranger Battalion at Green Lane Camp. The advance detachment consisted of Captain La Fountain, Captain Wood, 1st Lieutenant Minvielle, Master Sergeant Pierce, Sergeant Sanders, Staff Sergeant Giardina, Staff Sergeant Nally and Tec 5 Nixon. The party had left Fort Benning on 13 April 1944, arriving at Fort Hamilton, New York on 15 April where they underwent processing for overseas movement. The detachment sailed from New York Harbor on 18 April on the *Nieuw Amsterdam*. Leon Minvielle remembers watching the Statue of Liberty disappearing from view as one of the most depressing moments of his life. On board the *Niuew Amsterdam* six officers were billeted in each state room and they ate in the third class dining room, served by a waiter. They also had the facilities of a cocktail lounge. Leon remembers that the enlisted men did not fare so well. They ate lined up in the Grand Ball Room. The ship zig-zagged across the Atlantic and landed in the Firth of Clyde. The men disembarked at Gouroch on 26 April. They then travelled by train arriving at Leominster at midnight. From Leominster they were transported by trucks to Kington Camp No.1, which at the time, was a half built general hospital.

The detachment was kept busy for the next two weeks drawing equipment and vehicles from all parts of England. After two weeks the detachment left for Berrington Park where they intended to prepare the camp for the rest of the division. Due to unforeseen circumstances they were unable to carry this out and after four days returned to Kington.

Troop ship: Nieuw Amsterdam
(U.S. Naval Historical Center).

From here the detachment moved into Green Lane Camp in Leominster, still continuing to draw equipment and vehicles. Leon Minvielle remembers the camp. He recalls sleeping on a cot with straw mattress with a bedroll. He was so cold that he slept in his woollen underwear underneath the woollen blankets. During the two weeks that the men spent at the camp they were invited to local people's homes for lunch.

After its time at Green Lane Camp the advance detachment moved all vehicles and equipment to Tidworth Barracks. It took six days to complete the movement but all was ready by 15 June when the rest of the division arrived.

The 7th Armored Division, or 'Lucky Seventh' was assigned to Patton's Third Army and Patton addressed the men prior to their crossing. Leon Minvielle remembers that it seemed that every third word was the 'F' word. The Division Commander's Aid told Leon that Patton, dressed in his Eisenhower jacket with riding britches, crop and ivory handled pistols, had asked the Division Commander, Major General Sylvester, how he looked. Apparently General Sylvester had answered: 'You look like a God damned Jackass.' After the 7th had landed in France, Sylvester was demoted to Lieutenant Colonel (after the war he regained his original rank).

On 7 August the division left Tidworth Barracks and embarked on L.S.T.s at Southampton and Portsmouth. They landed along with their vehicles on Omaha and Utah Beach on 13-14 August 1944. The division was soon involved in action, attacking German troops in Chartres, Dreux and Melun. By the end of the month the division had liberated Chateau-Thierry and Verdun.

As the division moved towards Paris it was ordered to pull over to the side of the road to let the French 2nd Armoured Division, headed by General LeClerk, through to participate in the liberation of Paris. Leon Minvielle remembers noticing that all the French vehicles were loaded with singing girls.

CHAPTER 3 – THE LUCKY SEVENTH

The 7th continued its drive across France to Reims and Metz. Leon remembers that at night Germans would infiltrate the convoy, in an attempt to get back to Germany. He recalls that one night, at about 2 a.m, the column ground to a halt. An officer from the engineer platoon behind the 7th reported that he had counted twelve vehicles instead of the ten he was meant to have in the convoy. The last two vehicles were found to contain Germans who were then captured.

In September the 7th crossed the Moselle River and took part in the heavy fighting around Metz. Just outside Metz Leon remembers leaning over to tell the driver of his half track to follow the Colonel's jeep. As he stood up the jeep was blown up and he was knocked out by the concussion. When he came to he found that he was the only survivior of the half track. He was awarded a purple heart medal for the injuries he sustained. Fortunately his injuries were not too serious and he was able to continue with his division.

7th Armored Division Anti-tank covers a road near Vielsalm, Belgium 23/12/44 (U.S. Army Center of Military History).

7th Armored Division in temporary position near St Vith, Belgium (U.S. Army Center of Military History).

By the end of September the 7th had been transferred to the 9th Army and took part in Operation Market Garden. It had reached the banks of the River Roer when the Germans launched the Ardennes Offensive. The division was then transferred to the 1st Army and sent to St Vith where, while fighting a withdrawal action, it was able to slow up the German advance.

On New Year's Eve Leon was ordered to return to Division H.Q. He was joined by a colleague, Captain Dunn. They decided to go into Liege to 'find a restaurant, drink wine and eat steaks', even though Liege was off limits because of Buzz Bombs. Leon asked the driver to collect the two men from Liege at 1.00 a.m., which he did. After he had picked up the officers the driver drove as fast as he could out of Liege when a Buzz bomb hit the town. Leon remembers Dunn saying that if the war didn't end soon he wouldn't make it. He had already had a narrow escape when a German threw a hand grenade which bounced off his helmet. Leon assured Dunn that with his luck he would make it. The next day Dunn was killed by an 88mm while in his tank.

CHAPTER 3 – THE LUCKY SEVENTH

At the end of January St Vith was recaptured and the 7th started pushing its way through the Hurtgen Forest. It then moved to the Rhine where some of the American forces had been able to cross on the Remagen bridge before it collapsed. They formed a bridgehead and the 7th Armored lined up on the river bank firing in support. The division was crossed on a pontoon bridge and participated in the Ruhr Pocket collapse in April when the 58th Panzer Corps surrendered. The division were then sent north to the Baltic Sea where it made contact with the Russian Army just before the end of the war in Europe.

After the advance party of the 7th Armored Division had left Green Lane the 16th Field Artillery Observation Battalion arrived in Leominster. The 16th had been formed at Fort Bragg, North Carolina. They were an intelligence gathering unit with the motto 'Information Please' (a saying taken from a radio show). The 16th had sailed to Britain from New York on the British operated French liner, *The Louis Pasteur*. On this occasion the ship sailed alone, rather than as part of a convoy, and docked in Liverpool on 30 June 1944.

The unit spent two weeks in the nissen huts at Green Lane Camp while drawing equipment and vehicles and awaiting transfer to France. While in England the men trained alongside British troops on the Royal Artillery Ranges near Stonehenge. The personnel were surprised at how often the British stopped for tea. The Americans preferred the warm beer that they drank in pubs such as the Black Swan, which they called 'The Dirty Duck'. The men also enjoyed eating fish and chips in the Leominster chip shops. Some were invited into local people's homes where they enjoyed warm hospitality.

The Louis Pasteur (U.S. Naval Historical Center).

S.S. Amos G. Throop (U.S. Naval Historical Center).

On 14 July the battalion drew emergency rations, collected extra jerry cans of gasoline to attach to their vehicles and made a 'motor march' to Lopscombe Corner in Wiltshire.

On 15 August the unit boarded the liberty ship *The Amos G. Throop* at Southampton for the 60 mile crossing to France. When the ship landed at Omaha beach the men climbed down rope nets over the side of the ship. After landing the 16th moved to St Mere Eglise and down the Brittany peninsula, passing through St Lo to join the 29th Infantry Division at Brest.

Brest was very heavily defended by the German forces because of the submarine pens there. Allied planes attacked the city daily. The 16th witnessed an Allied fighter plane losing a wing and crashing over the city. The pilot ejected but his parachute didn't open and by the time medics from the 16th got to him he was already dead. Finally, after a longer battle than was expected, the Allied forces took Brest and the battalion crossed the bay to the Crognon Peninsula. As the battalion swept down the peninsula a large number of German prisoners were taken.

The 16th pushed forward until they reached Auw in Germany. On 16 December they came under heavy fire at their Command Point. On 17 December Captain Scarborough of the 285th Field Artillery Observer Battalion reported to the Commanding Officer of the 16th to request survey data and general instructions regarding the area around the 4th Infantry Division Artillery headquarters in Luxembourg, that they were heading for. On receiving the information Captain Scarborough set off leaving instructions for B Battery of the 285th, who were following behind, to be redirected to join the rest of the unit.

CHAPTER 3 – THE LUCKY SEVENTH

B Battery received their instructions from the 16th and left Schevenhutte at 0800 on 17 December, reaching Malmedy without incident. At Malmedy members of the 291st Engineer Combat Battalion advised the Battery to take a detour as German armour had been seen on the route they were taking. The unit was behind schedule and, to their cost, ignored the advice. As the 285th left Malmedy they met elements of the 7th Armored Division making towards St Vith. At the Baugnez crossroads the M.P. on duty who had recently directed the 7th Armored towards St Vith directed the 285th the other way, towards Ligneuville. As the convoy moved up the road towards Ligneuville they were met by German tanks that fired on them. Four of the Battery's trucks that had fallen behind the main body of the convoy heard the shooting and took evasive action, returning to Malmedy and thus escaping capture.

The survivors of the main convoy surrendered, except for five men who escaped. By 1400 hours around 113 American prisoners were assembled in a field, the number including 90 members of the 285th and the M.P. who had recently directed them. The prisoners were then fired upon by the Germans. Their bodies were not discovered until the Allied forces took back the area in January. However the bodies of eleven men of the 285th were not found until February and it is thought that they were forced to act as drivers of the serviceable American vehicles for the Germans until they too were shot in cold blood.

Meanwhile the 16th had found it necessary to retreat from their position, German patrols had cut the wire lines the men were using to send information and a number of forward observers had been captured. The battalion withdrew to St Vith and were attached to General Patton's 4th Armored Division for the push to Bastogne. From Bastogne the men moved back into Germany, past Auw to Saxony where they visited a liberated concentration camp. This experience had a profound effect on the men. Shortly after this the war in Europe ended and the unit regrouped ready for redeployment to the Pacific Theater of Operations.

Meanwhile the advance detachment of the 3187th Signal Service Battalion arrived in Leominster in early November 1944 and was joined by the rest of the Battalion on 30 December. For the first two nights the men were billeted in a barn at the Farmers Market. After this they were moved into accommodation in the town, possibly in Bargates.

David Finn of the 3187th remembers being billeted in a shop opposite the old library. He recalls that the shop was gutted to make space for six to eight cots.

Gene Overholt, a member of the advance detachment, remembers that there was no central heating or electricity in his billet and that it was necessary to heat water in a brick oven with a concrete basin on top and which had a small space below the basin to build a wood fire.

The men ate in a mess hall in the barn at the Farmers Market, Edward Moy remembers being so cold that he ate with his gloves on. David Finn also recalls that it was so foggy in the dark winter mornings that he had to find the mess hall by sound. He also remembers standing in formation in early morning fall out: *"cold, dark and miserable."*

3187th Signal Service Battalion – Ed Moy shown with arrow (E. Moy).

CHAPTER 3 – THE LUCKY SEVENTH

3187th in formation in Leominster (E. Moy).

Edward Moy recalls that the only food to be bought in the shops was bread, which the men ate with jam from the mess hall for an evening snack. He remembers going to the cinema in the week and dances, attended by the Land Army girls from Bircher Hall, at the weekends. The men also had time for sightseeing trips to London, Birmingham and Coventry. In Coventry they were shocked to see the devastation caused by the Blitz.

Some men were given three day passes. Bob Angell remembers visiting his cousin in the U.S. Army Air Force who took him to visit some distant English cousins who ran a pub in London. One of the relatives gave him a bottle of gin. Once back in Leominster Bob and some of his colleagues decided to have proper bath instead of the sponge baths they had been having up to that time. Three of the men heated up 15 gallons of hot water and took it upstairs to the bathroom which had no heating. Bob recalls:

"How many of us took a bath I can't remember but I took one and got pneumonia."

To avoid him going off sick the rest of the men plied Bob with the hot gin, piled on the blankets and let him sweat it out for several days. Bob swears that this kept him out of hospital and let him remain with the unit.

The unit left Leominster on 2 February 1945. They travelled to Southampton and then sailed to France. The unit travelled through France to Germany where they became part of the Army of Occupation for nine months before travelling home.

CHAPTER 4

A DIAMOND IN THE ROUGH (76TH GENERAL HOSPITAL)

Before the infantry, ordnance and armoured units began to arrive at Leominster plans had been put forward to build a 1000 bed general hospital at Barons Cross, on the outskirts of the town. The hospital would fulfil two roles, it would act as a station hospital for troops stationed in Leominster and the vicinity and also as a general hospital for the injured from combat in Europe after D-Day. For this purpose the Ministry of Defence requisitioned the land around Barons Cross including part of the Cornhill Cop Farm, which was tenanted by the Sanders family. Building work was commenced at the beginning of 1943.

Gertrude Cox worked on the site as a cook catering for the building contractors. She was responsible for providing a midday and evening meal for the men. Other local ladies served the meals and cooked the breakfasts. Every day, except Sunday, a coach collected Gertrude and other ladies from Stourport on Severn, where they lived, and took them to the Barons Cross site. Because Gertrude's two daughters were too young to be left at home she took them with her on Saturdays.

The first hospital to arrive at Plant 4177 was the 76th General Hospital. This unit had been activated at Camp White, Oregon on 28 September 1942 and was commanded by Colonel Paul S. Fancher. After two months of basic training the 76th moved to Vancouver, Washington, where it was attached to Barnes General Hospital for completion of basic training and for technical training.

On 19 February 1944 an advance party of two officers and three enlisted men travelled to Boston P.O.E. and sailed for Llandudno, Wales arriving on 29 February. At Llandudno a staging area was being set up for hospitals arriving in England and awaiting completion of, or vacancies of, sites.

Meanwhile the rest of the unit prepared for the long train journey through Washington, Idaho, Montana, the Dakotas, Minnesota, Iowa, Illinois, Indiana, Ohio, Pennsylvania, New York, Vermont and Massachusetts to the staging area at Camp Miles Standish. Doc Laborde remembers spending the week with his parents before travelling to the staging area. On his return to Vancouver the men were issued with khaki (summer) uniforms so deployment to the Pacific Theater of Operations was anticipated. In the middle of the night on 14 February, with no prior notice, the men were instructed to pack their barracks bags and assemble ready to march to Vancouver Train Station. On reaching Camp Miles Standish the khaki uniforms were swapped for the regular army winter uniforms.

On 27 February the men set out to the Boston P.O.E. where they boarded the troop ship, *U.S.A.T. George Washington*. At 0500 hours on 28 February the transport ship set sail as part of a convoy from Boston Harbor. After eleven days at sea the convoy dropped anchor in the Irish Sea near the mouth of the River Mersey and the following day docked at Liverpool. After disembarking the unit travelled by train to Llandudno, where a hospital staging area had just been opened. The advance party had made all the arrangements for the 76th in the town.

U.S.A.T. George Washington (U.S. Naval Historical Center).

CHAPTER 4 – A DIAMOND IN THE ROUGH

At this newly opened staging area, while billeted in private dwellings, the 76th General Hospital was orientated to life in Great Britain. During the two weeks the personnel spent here they attended lectures and acquired some of the vehicles needed for the Motor Transportation Section of the hospital.

On 23 March the advance party, consisting of two officers and 20 enlisted men and designated 'Detachment A', was sent to Barons Cross to prepare for the arrival of the main body. At the same time Detachment B consisting of 16 officers, 12 nurses and 125 enlisted men, set off for a temporary assignment at Clough, Northern Ireland, where they were to operate a station hospital. On 29 March the remainder of the 76th left by train for Barons Cross, arriving on the same day.

On arrival at Barons Cross the personnel were surprised to find that the site was still very much under construction. The archivist for the 76th describes its appearance as: "A diamond in the rough". He continues the description:

"And in the rough it was with its 35 acres, its permanent buildings and 14 contractor's buildings ... the grounds for the most part stripped of sod, were littered with refuse, contractor's supplies and tools. Two hundred British workmen were on site, going in and out of these buildings in the endless task of completing the finishing touches. These workmen were [still] living in the buildings which were to be the enlisted men's quarters and were using the enlisted men's mess. In many places the cement in the walls, roofs and also that used in sealing the windows and doors of the buildings had already cracked and commenced to crumble. Many of the roofs leaked and much of the plasterboard used in sealing the wards had dried out and become detached from the framework. Much of the plumbing, which was of a very poor quality and also poorly installed, required repair or replacement. Every faucet and every toilet leaked. While the natural slope of the site facilitated drainage no attempt had been made to divert the flow of surface water from the buildings. The few ditches already present were overgrown and filled with rubbish. In the lower part of the area were five stagnant pools, excellent breeding places for mosquitoes." (76th General Hospital Archives)

However the main problem that faced the 76th General Hospital was that the entire plant had been built on a British design for an 834 bed British hospital with adequate facilities for personnel and equipment for a 750 bed (station) hospital, when it was a 1000 bed (general) hospital that was required. The archivist for the 76th comments:

Aerial view of Barons Cross 1946 (reproduced with the permission of English Heritage).

CHAPTER 4 – A DIAMOND IN THE ROUGH

"A 1000 bed general hospital with its personnel, additional departments, supplies and equipment had to be 'shoe-horned' into the existing facility. The main problems involved were but a challenge to a unit anxious to perform the mission for which it was organised and trained." (76th General Hospital Archives)

It was necessary for the Commanding Officer to solve the problems that were before him. First he looked into the space for patients in existing wards. The hospital currently had twenty eight 38-bed wards and one 14-bed ward making a total of 854 beds. It was decided that spaces in the centre of the wards could be utilised if necessary for an extra 146 beds. By 1 June 22 ward tents had been erected on the end of wards and were fully equipped thus making a total of 1184 available beds.

Part of Ministry of Works plans for Barons Cross showing that it was built as a 750 bed hospital (Herefordshire Records Office).

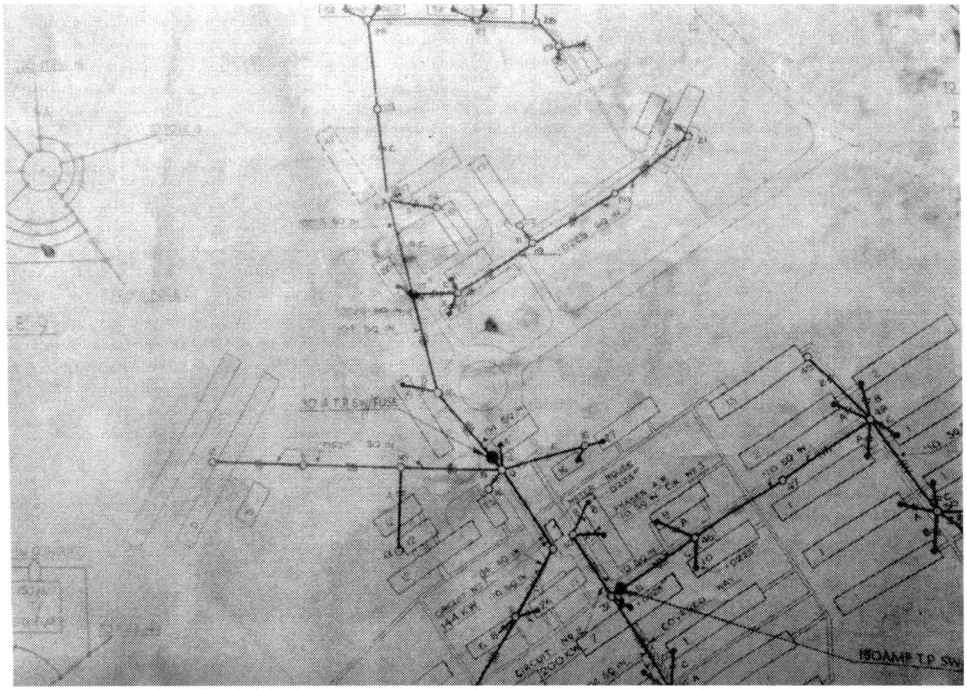

Part of Ministry of Works plans for Barons Cross (Herefordshire Records Office).

Discussions were then conducted with the contractor as to how the building work on site could be completed more quickly and efficiently and also what adaptations there would need to be to buildings so that there was the correct amount of facilities for a 1000 bed hospital. It would be necessary to change the use of some of the buildings from their designations on the original construction plans. The contractor agreed to carry out the necessary changes and additions to the existing buildings in exchange for the unit's assuming responsibility for cleaning the buildings, policing the grounds and completing all landscaping.

It was decided that each department in the hospital was to be given responsibility for their own building, adapting them for purpose and installing the required equipment. In addition departments were to take responsibility for cleaning and landscaping the areas surrounding the buildings.

On the hospital site there were 65 permanent hospital buildings which were brick built with dividing walls made of red hollow tiles and roofs made of asbestos. Some

CHAPTER 4 – A DIAMOND IN THE ROUGH

buildings could be modified to house more than one department; the Outpatients Department was established in the Receiving and Evacuation building and operated by the same personnel. Another building was used both for the X-ray clinic and Physiotherapy Department. A centrally located building intended for a tailor and cobbler's shop was used for a combination post office and barbers shop.

Two buildings were assigned to the laboratory; the one was a large clinical laboratory unit which was adapted to accommodate the pharmacy as well as the laboratory. This meant that the large building intended for pharmacy and pharmacy stores could be used for the offices of the Registrar, the Commanding Officer of the Detachment of Patients and the Personnel Section. The smaller laboratory building, which was a morgue, was unused by the 76th for its original purpose.

The motor pool for the hospital consisted of a mechanics shed, fully equipped for first and second echelon maintenance, a dispatchers office, a wash and grease rack and a large cement parking area.

There were five messes on site, each consisting of separate cookhouses and a mess hall. One of the cookhouses had an electric warming oven while the other four were equipped with coal burning ranges. All ranges had to be reset and insulated prior to use. At first, due to the scattered locations and lack of personnel, only three of the messes were utilised, one for the officers, one for the enlisted personnel and one for patients. It was necessary to adapt the patients mess by putting in more doorways. The extra doorways were to enable the food carts, which were loaded with meals and special diets for bed patients, to be moved to the wards without disrupting the queue of ambulatory patients waiting for food. It was necessary to organise a rota of sittings for the ambulatory patients as the mess only took 350 at one time. Ambulatory patients would queue for meals in a covered walkway with a roof but no sides.

Dishwashing in the mess hall was also a problem due to the lack of hot water. A dishwashing machine was requisitioned but never arrived. There were two large boilers which were kept constantly filled with boiling water for washing and all food utensils were immersed in a sterilising solution as a final precaution.

The water supply for the hospital came from wells in Leominster. It was found to need chlorination once it arrived at the hospital. It was necessary to chlorinate the water by hand in the 58000 gallon storage tank. A drip chlorinator was requisitioned by the hospital but never arrived. A sewage plant was erected a quarter of a mile from the hospital grounds.

The hospital had various systems for reducing waste. Rainwater was used where possible. Mess areas were supervised to keep food wastage to a minimum. Garbage was collected daily by a local farmer. Grease was collected from grease traps, refined and given to a salvage agency. Cardboard boxes were turned over to British salvage agencies. Paper and envelopes were reused, dressings were reclaimed and reused, damaged equipment and linens were mended whenever possible. Cans and other unsalvageable trash and paper were crushed and hauled to a local dump.

In addition to the 65 permanent buildings the fourteen temporary contractor's shacks were utilised, two for utilities shops, six for storage and two for the British workmen remaining on site. Some 35 civilian personnel were employed at the hospital. Thirteen were workman employed to upkeep the fabric of the buildings. This number included a foreman, electrician, plumber, pipe fitter, carpenter, sewage attendant, three boiler attendants and four stokers. The remaining 22 staff was used to increment the military personnel, two were gardeners, two were labourers, there were four switchboard operators, three stenographers, two seamstresses and nine cleaners.

It was necessary for the four remaining temporary buildings to be utilised as enlisted mens' billets as the original provision on site was inadequate. The permanent living quarters were in buildings measuring 20 by 30 feet. They had cement floors and sidewalls and the roofs were made of asbestos. Ventilation was through windows and ventilators. Each hut contained a coal burning stove. The officers had nine huts and the nurses fourteen. (The five Red Cross workers were billeted with the nurses). There were twenty huts for the enlisted men and it was necessary to put nine or ten bunks in each to fit the men in.

The ablutions buildings in the officers', nurses' and non-commissioned officers' areas also contained shower and toilet facilities while in the enlisted mens' area there were separate buildings for each function. Local firms were contracted to carry out laundry for the 76th but unfortunately they were not equipped to handle the quantity of laundry supplied by the hospital so laundry tubs were installed in ablution buildings for hospital personnel to do their own laundry. Utilisation was also made of transient American portable laundry units in the vicinity.

The Red Cross operated two buildings on the hospital site, one a Recreation Hall, which was used as a craft shop and games room, and the other a building housing a library, officer patient's lounge, kitchen, storeroom and the Assistant Field Director's Office.

CHAPTER 4 – A DIAMOND IN THE ROUGH

On 8 April supplies for the hospital were released. Although the 76th were anxious to obtain the supplies so that the hospital could function efficiently, there was little space on site to store the supplies. On their arrival the personnel had found three of the ward buildings filled with unrequisitioned British supplies and the assigned warehouses were still occupied by the British contractors and their equipment.

The Medical Supply Section was responsible for cataloguing all supplies and distributing those that could be utilised throughout the hospital, moving the balance to less essential buildings. Because of the lack of storage space it became necessary to tally out the unit equipment to the respective wards, departments and clinics immediately upon its arrival. Stock records could not be established until requisitions were received and distributed. This delayed the requisitioning of shortages and the replacement of expendable items.

Equipment for the hospital had been stored at a supply depot 45 miles away from the hospital (Honeybourne). The supply depot transported twenty loads of equipment and then informed the hospital that no more transport was available for the further 432 loads by rail or truck and that:

"If the hospital desired early delivery of the remainder of the assemblage it would have to assume responsibility for its transportation." (76th General Hospital Archives)

It was necessary for the hospital to use their own trucks and 'borrow' trucks from units in Leominster to collect the remainder of the equipment. Fortunately the personnel were able to borrow six trucks from a transportation unit and by working day and night they were able to collect all of the equipment within 10 days. Some equipment arrived damaged but most of it could be repaired locally.

The carpentry shop were able to salvage crating and packing material from the new supplies to make equipment needed throughout the hospital such as racks, cabinets and shelving. They also made stands for the fire fighting equipment and bulletin boards for the wards. The carpentry shop also made first aid boxes for all of the vehicles.

The hospital was to encounter problems with supply even after if had opened to patients. Many supplies had been earmarked for D-Day and could not be used prior to the event. The hospital found that it was often necessary to contact four or five depots to locate certain scarce items and then provide transport to collect them. Another problem was procuring clothing and equipment in sufficient quantity for patients being discharged from the hospital. Medical forms were another item in short supply and it was necessary to mimeograph the back of forms used. After D-Day the supply situation was somewhat relieved and forms were more plentiful.

The various departments worked hard to prepare their buildings and the surrounding area. The general landscaping and preparation of individual quarters was carried out by officers, nurses and enlisted men working individually and together at all hours of the day. The unit had the use of a bulldozer for three days (lent by an engineer unit); apart from this all landscaping and clearing of debris was carried out by hand. The archivist records:

Barons Cross Hospital Site (76th General Hospital Archives).

CHAPTER 4 – A DIAMOND IN THE ROUGH

"Trees and hedges were neatly trimmed, ditches cleared, water pumped from stagnant pools which were then filled with the rubbish, rock and dirt from the hospital area. Trees and shrubbery were planted and grass seed sown ... All the personnel worked feverishly, some were building cupboards, shelving, desks and numerous improvisations, others were sanding, varnishing and painting while the remainder were distributing and installing hospital equipment and supplies."
(76th General Hospital Archives)

By the end of April the Stars and Stripes was ready to be hoisted up the newly erected flagpole and flown. A formal retreat was held and the hospital was officially opened.
After an inspection on 11 June the Surgeon, Western Base Section reported:

"Of all the units under my command the 76th General Hospital is one of two hospitals which have accomplished the most in the shortest period of time."
(76th General Hospital Archives)

CHAPTER 5

A JOB WELL DONE
(76TH GENERAL HOSPITAL)

Prior to D-Day the 76th General Hospital functioned mainly as a station hospital, treating staff from the hospital and troops billeted in Leominster. An outpatient clinic was set up and it was recorded that:

"The most common traumatic conditions treated in the outpatient clinic from members of the command were those resulting from bicycle accidents." (76th General Hospital Archives)

At 2.30 a.m., a few days after D-Day, hospital personnel were called to duty to prepare for the first trainload of combat casualties. Patients were to arrive by rail at Leominster Station, approximately two miles from the hospital. The first convoy of patients to be received were paratroopers from the D-Day invasion. Nurse Mary Roberson remembers:

"It was like the whole country opened up and came in our door. The ambulances were door to door. It was a terrible experience. They were young men, some weren't 20."

The hospital was to specialise in orthopaedics and 70% of the patients received after D-Day needed orthopaedic treatment or had an orthopaedic condition in addition

CHAPTER 5 – A JOB WELL DONE

to other wounds. A significant number of the parachute and airborne infantry troops had suffered fractures on landing.

One of the casualties was George Davis, a glider pilot who had taken off from Membury, Wiltshire in the early hours of 6 June. On 10 June he was evacuated to Barons Cross where he spent four months recovering. After a further month at a convalescent hospital in Bromsgrove, where he received the Purple Heart, he returned to active duty at Membury. Another patient was Gordon Greenlaw who had gone ashore on D-Day and had been wounded in the leg at Labell, France. After an operation on his leg to remove the bullet he was hospitalised for several months before being sent to the Zone of the Interior to be honourably discharged. He was awarded the Bronze Star and Purple Heart.

For the main part casualties had been given preliminary treatment at a first aid station or field hospital before being evacuated to the U.K. and boarded onto a train. Hospital trains were unloaded either on the main platform at Leominster or from the siding. When it was possible to unload on the main platform the average train could be unloaded in between 30 and 75 minutes depending on the number of litter cases and the type of train. Unloading from the siding presented several problems which the hospital eventually solved: tracks often had to be reset to accommodate heavier trains; it was necessary to clear the siding of freight cars each time a train arrived; a delay was caused by the fact that the ambulance road did not extend the full length of the siding.

When these problems had been resolved unloading time from the siding was reduced from three hours to one and a half. Plans were put into place to evacuate patients by train after treatment but during the period that the 76th were at Barons Cross all evacuations were by motor convoy.

Initially fourteen wards were assigned to the Surgical Service but following D-Day it was realised that battle casualties were likely to be 90% surgical cases. It then became necessary to assign to the Surgical Service eight additional wards from the Medical Service and 18 of the 22 ward tents. It was also necessary to assign five officers from the Medical Service to the Surgical Service full time and two officers part time.

Fortunately, soon after the opening of the hospital a course in anaesthesia had been inaugurated for selected nurses. Once the trainloads of casualties arrived at the hospital it was found that the original number of anaesthetists was insufficient and it was necessary to put the newly qualified nurses to use straight away.

Above: *G.I on Leominster Station* (Kington Camp Project).

Left: *Nurse Marcella Ryan Lebeau* (76th General Hospital).

CHAPTER 5 – A JOB WELL DONE

Before D-Day, while the hospital was functioning as a station hospital, elective surgery was not carried out on cases not expected to return to duty within 90 days. After D-Day the 90 day rule still stood but cases were classified into three groups:

1. Those who would return to duty after treatment.

2. Those who would be transferred to a rehabilitation centre before returning to duty.

3. Those who were to return to the Zone of the Interior.

The system necessitated continuous classification and reclassification as the condition and therefore status of the patient changed.

Initially twelve wards were assigned to the Medical Service of the hospital but after D-Day five of them were transferred for the use of the Surgical Service. A large number of surgical cases did have medical conditions, such as pulmonary and cardiac complications occurring in wounds of the chest, requiring treatment from the Medical Service. There were no patient deaths while the 76th were at Barons Cross but there were a large number of critically ill patients. Gas gangrene of the extremities was suffered by some patients, severe cases needed amputation.

Some surgical patients were also found to have neuropsychiatric conditions, 80 patients were admitted to the Neuropsychiatric Section of the Medical Service while the 76th were at Barons Cross. Some 42 proved to be cases of psychoneurosis, 10 psychoses, 22 psychopathic personality, three mental deficiency and three epilepsy. Narcosis therapy was used in some newly developed cases of profound anxiety neurosis. Insulin therapy plus narcosis was used in twelve cases of long standing neurosis.

Working alongside the medical and surgical departments of the hospital were three non-medical organisations. The archivist for the 76th comments:

"The success in welfare, social service and recreational activities which this unit has enjoyed is attributed to the close operation between these departments and the coordination of their respective programmes." (76th General Hospital Archives)

The Chaplain's Department consisted of a Protestant Chaplain and assistant and a Catholic Chaplain and assistant. One of the officers in the unit who was the son of a Rabbi, provided Jewish services and another officer assumed responsibility for conducting services for a group of Adventists.

The Special Services Department of the 76th provided educational and recreational activities. They were directed and coordinated by one officer and one non-commissioned officer. They would often request the services of other officers and enlisted men in the 76th to supervise some of the activities.

As well as recreational activities the Special Services administered training to the personnel in both military and professional subjects. Special emphasis was given to military courtesy and discipline, care of individual clothing and equipment, chemical welfare and gas mask drill, litter drill and ambulance loading. The personnel also had weekly fire drills and periodic air raid drills. They simulated the reception and treatment of gas casualties and just prior to the opening of the hospital they took part in a simulation of the admission and evacuation of a large number of patients in a short period of time.

The Red Cross Unit consisted of five workers. Two of them went with Detachment B to Northern Ireland from Llandudno and rejoined the unit at Barons Cross later. The Red Cross activities of the hospital were installed in two large buildings, one of which housed the library, lounge, office and supply room, while the other housed the theatre, games room and craft shop.

The Red Cross staff had some problems to overcome when setting up their programmes. At the beginning of June there were only three girls to carry out the work and their equipment had not yet arrived. As soon as Special Service material arrived it was given to the Red Cross to distribute among the wards.

On arrival in Leominster the Red Cross started to make links with the local community. Martha Wolk (A.F.D.) states in her first report:

> *"We find the people of the community very much interested in our programme – their help is greatly appreciated."* (76th General Hospital Archives)

A number of local people were willing to invite recovering patients to their homes for visits and meals. The Red Cross made the contacts in the town and then made lists of patients who would benefit from such visits.

The Red Cross aimed to provide flowers for the wards, a library and some of the offices. The girls made arrangements with the proprietress of the local flower shop, Mrs Hunt, to provide flowers for the hospital and also with another shopkeeper, Mrs

CHAPTER 5 – A JOB WELL DONE

Page, who agreed to have flowers left in her shop by local people for the hospital. Ambulances were sent out to collect the flowers every Friday. Too many flowers were received for the Red Cross to arrange so it was necessary to enlist the help of patients. One patient, a sailor who was formerly a florist, was happy to take on the task. At first the Red Cross had to rely on a local hotel to lend vases to arrange the flowers in while a neighbour contributed a beautiful old Wedgewood vase. Eventually the girls managed to find a supplier of vases.

The Red Cross also enlisted the help of the W.V.S. to organise a group of ladies to attend the Recreation Hall once a week to sew and mend for patients and personnel. One of the hospital's neighbours, a blind First World War veteran, offered to come and teach the patients rug working in the craft shop.

A craft programme was available to patients both on the ward and in the craft shop. The craft shop in the Recreation Hall was busy every afternoon. The men had the opportunity to try their hand at leather work, woodwork, metal work, linoleum printing, plexiglass, lanyards and needlework. A number of the men made articles in felt such as comfort bags. The patients could also use tin cans salvaged from the mess hall to make ash trays and bed tags. Some patients enjoyed drawing, painting or making clay models. A number of traction bed patients on the wards became interested in leatherwork and belt making.

The Red Cross organised visits to the hospital by various individuals and groups. At one point Joe Louis visited the hospital, had lunch with the patients and visited each ward. Another group of visitors that were popular with the patients were the seven 5-month old collie puppies living on the post. On several occasions the puppies paid 'ward calls' and they also visited the Recreation Hall frequently. The girls also had a kitten aptly named 'E.T.O.'. The Red Cross unit for the 135th took over the care of the animals when the 76th left. The A.F.D. of the 135th also noted that the patients enjoyed petting the dogs and many commented on how similar they were to their own pets at home.

In cooperation with the Special Services the theatre was used for Red Cross Performances and U.S.O. shows. The hospital had several visits from a group called 'Sweet and Swing' whose programmes were short but well planned. The Red Cross organised some shows themselves. 'Amateur Nights' were a form of talent show which: ...

"... revealed considerable talent as well as fun."

Joe Louis visiting a hospital in England (U.S. Military Archives).

One musician impressed the Red Cross staff by playing the guitar and harmonica together by using a wire contraption around his neck to hold the harmonica in place. The girls also found the magician who made their watches disappear entertaining.

Each month the Red Cross organised a 'birthday party' in the theatre for patients with a birthday in that month. Movies were also shown in the theatre. At the beginning it was necessary to borrow a projector to use but when Special Services had one delivered it was possible to set out a weekly schedule of movies shown in the theatre and also sometimes on the wards for bed patients.

On 22 May the hospital was given notice that it would be assigned to Forward Echelon, Communication Zone, although it would remain for administrative purposes under the Western Base Section for the time being. This was the first intimation that the unit was earmarked for continental duties. On 31 May Detachment B joined the 76th at Barons Cross from Northern Ireland to prepare

CHAPTER 5 – A JOB WELL DONE

for movement to the continent. At the beginning of June notification was received of the transfer of the 76th to Advance Section, Communication Zone. Along with the transfer came directives for 'Preparation for Short Overseas Voyage'. This meant that in addition to continuing day to day work in the hospital, preparation was to be made for movement at short notice. It was necessary to stream line personal equipment so that excesses could be packed and stored in the U.K. or shipped to the Zone of the Interior. Plans were made and rehearsed for breaking down essential housekeeping and administrative equipment and supplies into vehicular loads. Designated organisational equipment was shipped to the depot to be added to the unit assemblage and motor vehicles were thoroughly overhauled. On 14 June Martha Wolk visited the Red Cross Headquarters in London to discuss the unit's imminent movement overseas and ask for advice on which Red Cross supplies she should take.

On 10 July the 76th were informed by telephone that the 135th General Hospital would be arriving at Barons Cross on 12 July and that it would be necessary to move the main body of the 76th General Hospital to a concentration area the following day. A rear party consisting of 10 officers, 10 nurses and 30 enlisted men were designated to remain to orient the new unit. The archives for the 76th record:

"On the morning of the 13th it was a proud organization of 'veterans' who made their farewell march around the flagpole and with emotions both of regret and anticipation, but with the knowledge of a job well done, entrained for a new assignment." (76th General Hospital Archives)

CHAPTER 6

THE BATTLE OF GENERAL MUD (76TH GENERAL HOSPITAL)

On 13 July 1945 the 76th General Hospital detrained at Pinkney Park, Wiltshire to stage at the tented encampment there. The 30th General Hospital, which was also staging in the area, had prepared a section of the camp and a hot meal for the 76th. After 48 hours at the camp field training, including courses in conversational French, was initiated. Special Services and Red Cross personnel organised entertainment on the base and daily 'liberty trucks' to Bristol, Bath and Swindon. Some personnel were given leave.

On 8 August all personnel were recalled and on 11 August the unit set off for a marshalling area near Eastleigh, Hampshire. During the next 36 hours British money was exchanged for French currency, embarkation rosters were checked and emergency rations issued.

On the morning of 13 August the 76th embarked on the *S.S. Nieuw Holland* and in the late afternoon the ship set off as part of a convoy across the Channel. The motor convoy, which had assembled at an adjoining area, had shipped out 24 hours earlier on a Liberty ship and arrived on the continent in sufficient time to act as an advance party for the rest of the unit.

Because of high seas it was necessary for the personnel to spend 72 hours aboard the *Nieuw Holland* in very cramped conditions. On the morning of the 16 August the landing barge came alongside the ship and, as the 76th had been last to board,

CHAPTER 6 – THE BATTLE OF GENERAL MUD

it was the first to disembark. That evening the whole unit was reunited in a bivouac area in a 'cow pasture' on the Cherbourg to Paris highway between Carentan and Isigny, eight miles from the landing point.

Unfortunately, and to their frustration, the 76th remained in the bivouac area for six weeks while they awaited the arrival of their equipment which, because of priority shipments, had been detained in Britain. In the last week of September the equipment arrived and on 29 September the advance party set off in motor vehicles for Paris. On the afternoon of the 29 September the personnel endured a 54 hour train journey to join them in Pairs. The following day the rear party closed the camp and followed with the remaining vehicles.

The 76th remained just outside Paris until 8 October then departed for Liege, Belgium. On arrival their orders were to set up a hospital to be ready to receive 450 patients in ten days. The hospital was to be a 'holding hospital' and it was anticipated that patients would be evacuated between 24 to 72 hours from the time of their admission. The exception to the rule would be those who could be returned to duty within ten days and those cases whose physical condition precluded their evacuation.

The hospital was to be tented with concrete bases. Unfortunately the engineers had commenced laying bases without consulting the medical staff. This meant that the layout was not as the personnel would have wished.

On 10 October orders were given to abandon the original plans for a tent surgery and to commence construction of a pavilion using prefabricated German building material. Unfortunately torrential rain slowed down the building process but by 17 October the hospital had 554 beds for use and facilities for their reception and care. Whilst the hospital was not fully complete it was adequate for emergency use. However due to the failure to construct roads and hard standings at the initial stage of the building development the hospital was awash with mud and it was impossible for ambulances to enter the area. The hospital officially opened as a 940 bed holding hospital on 1 November 1944.

On 4 November fifty German Prisoners of War were assigned to work at the hospital. They were put to work on maintenance of the roads and walkways; kitchen labour duties; litter bearers; sanitary police and various unit and supply details. By 13 November 150 more prisoners had arrived at the hospital and they were later joined by a further 200. They were housed in shelter tents in a stockade about a quarter of a mile from the hospital and were held under the administration of the 1864th Labor Supervision company. The stockade was constructd by the prisoners themselves.

Laying concrete bases in Enlisted Mens' quarters (76th General Hospital Archives).

The principal problems encountered in the use of German prisoners were disciplinary issues. An organised movement among certain of the prisoners to discourage anything more than the minimum amount of labour and effort from the prisoners was discovered and resulted in the return of the leaders of the movement to the Central Advance Section Stockade. Several infractions of discipline occurred, sometimes involving the rebelling of some privates against their own non-commissioned officers. Eight prisoners escaped during this period, two groups of three cut their way out of the stockade at night before the double row of barbed wire, sentry towers and lighting system were completed. Two prisoners escaped from the Utilities Section during the day.

Because the hospital received patients more directly from the front line there were a number of deaths at the hospital. From November to December 1944 the Surgical Service had 23 deaths, most of this number dying within 24 hours of arriving at the hospital. All those that died had multiple wounds. The Medical Service had only one death, which was from myeloblastic leukemia.

CHAPTER 6 – THE BATTLE OF GENERAL MUD

Pathway named after Commanding Officer (76th General Hospital Archives).

76th General Hospital in Liege Winter 1944 (Courtesy of WW2 U.S. Medical Research Center – www.med-dept.com).

German prisoners working on the grounds at the hospital (76th General Hospital Archives).

CHAPTER 6 – THE BATTLE OF GENERAL MUD

Admitting patients at Receiving office (76th General Hospital Archives).

From November to December 831 cases were admitted to the Neuropsychaiatric section of the hospital. Most of these were suffering from 'combat exhaustion' and very few could be returned to duty in less than ten days so they were evacuated to a hospital that could treat them for a longer period.

On the morning of 17 April a V1 rocket hit the 76th General Hospital. Fortunately it struck midway between the Motor Pool and a section of the enlisted mens' quarters on the exit road from the hospital and no personnel were killed, although two officers and 34 enlisted men received minor injuries from shrapnel and flying debris. None of the personnel needed hospitalisation for longer than 48 hours. However damage to equipment was extensive. The laboratory, pharmacy, E.E.N.T. and dental clinics, surgery, Special Services building and Motor Pool sustained damage. All equipment was either repaired or replaced within 24 hours so that the running of the hospital was only slightly affected.

Dodge WC51 truck delivering meals to wards (76th General Hospital Archives).

General panorama of wards (76th General Hospital Archives).

CHAPTER 6 – THE BATTLE OF GENERAL MUD

Left: *Nurses corner of ward* (76th General Hospital Archives).

Below: *Detachment Officer at Bulletin board* (76th General Hospital Archives).

On 26 December there was another incident when a German plane strafed the area of the nurses quarters at around 2320 hours. Two tents were hit by shell fire, one being the living quarters of the Chief Nurse, in which she was sleeping at the time. Fortunately the only damage consisted of small shell holes in two tents and a small amount of damage to personal clothes and possessions. There seemed to be no obvious reason for the attack as the night was clear and moonlit and the red Geneva Crosses could clearly be seen on top of the tents.

Christmas festivities marked the end of 1944 thanks to the efforts of the Red Cross. Wards and Departments were supplied with Christmas decorations made by wounded Belgian soldiers and school children. On Christmas Eve the Red Cross organised a Bingo Party with cigarette prizes. This was followed by cider and

76th Orchestra – 'Swinging Out' (76th General Hospital Archives).

CHAPTER 6 – THE BATTLE OF GENERAL MUD

Geneva crosses to be clearly seen on tents. Photo taken while laying concrete bases in enlisted mens' area (76th General Hospital Archives).

doughnuts. The party ended with carols sung by a group that the Chaplain had organised. As the patients left at 10.00 a group of officer patients arrived so the girls entertained them with playing cards. At 11.00 they made a large pot of coffee for the men but at that moment the wardman arrived to collect the patients who were to be evacuated. Just as the girls were wondering what to do with the coffee more officer patients arrived, the wardman had rounded up more men to drink the ready made coffee.

On Christmas Day all patients received a Red Cross present as well as cigarettes and candy. The girls had ordered a Santa suit for Sergeant Gale, the enlisted man assigned to the Red Cross, but when the box was opened a St Nicholas costume was found inside with purple satin tunic, a chasable of red velvet, white shoes, stockings and gloves. Sergeant Gale agreed to wear the costume and as Martha Wolk stated:

"It would be good for a laugh – something we all needed." (76th General Hospital Archives)

On Christmas Day afternoon Martha drove St Nicholas around the hospital area distributing presents and leaflets about the history of the region around Liege. The costume had a mitre of white satin which Sergeant Gale wore at alternate times with his steel helmet.

The function of the hospital from January to May 1945 was more like that of an evacuation hospital rather than a general hospital. The function of an evacuation hospital was to admit large numbers of battle casualties, administrate necessary surgical or medical treatment and prepare patients for further evacuation to the rear. During January to May 11, 416 American military personnel were admitted to the hospital.

Smoke rising after V1 explosion (76th General Hospital Archives).

CHAPTER 6 – THE BATTLE OF GENERAL MUD

Aftermath of the V1 explosion (76th General Hospital Archives).

From 17 December the City of Liege had been subject to an almost constant barrage of V1 rockets and by the end of December troops of the German counter offensive had reached a point about twelve miles from the city. Tentative plans were made to evacuate the hospital if it became necessary to abandon the area. As the front line moved nearer to the hospital the patient load became heavier. At one point patients were evacuated directly to the hospital from the field of battle. The peak came on 3 February when 448 patients were admitted on the one day.

On 8 January another V1 rocket landed on the hospital. This time it landed in the midst of four tents filled with sleeping guards and laundry section personnel. Some 25 enlisted men were killed and fourteen wounded as well as one Belgian civilian. Damage to hospital buildings and equipment was extensive.

Left: *Aftermath of the V1 explosion* (76th General Hospital Archives).

Below: *Buzz bomb damage to vehicles* (76th General Hospital Archives).

CHAPTER 6 – THE BATTLE OF GENERAL MUD

Above: *Buzz bomb damage to vehicles* (76th General Hospital Archives).

Right: *Plaque erected on flagpole base* (76th General Hospital Archives).

In February the 76th took part in a project run by the Servicemen's Christian League to adopt Belgian children. Two children, a boy of 12 and a girl of 11, whose fathers had been killed by the Gestapo for their activities in the resistance movement, were adopted by the unit. The goal of 500 Belgian Francs for each child was met and surpassed. Extra money was turned over to a women's committee for the relief of war victims to help other unfortunate children. Twice a week the two adopted children visited the post and received gifts from various members of the personnel.

By the middle of February the situation in the Battle of the Bulge had changed in the Allies' favour and the rate of admissions of patients slowed down. In March the 76th were able to carry out some reconstruction on the hospital site. The archivist comments:

Orphan outside post-Theatre after sustaining damage from V1 hit (76th General Hospital Archives).

CHAPTER 6 – THE BATTLE OF GENERAL MUD

"The Battle of General Mud, one of the major campaigns of the Winter, was no longer a deterrent to improving the hospital area so an extensive programme of reseeding, landscaping and building was instituted." (76th General Hospital Archives)

Towards the end of March the Battle of the Ruhr Pocket caused another large influx of casualties but this dropped at the end of April and continued dropping until V.E. Day. In April a number of released American prisoners of war were admitted to the hospital. Most had evidence of weight loss varying from twenty to sixty pounds and exhibited other manifestations of malnutrition which persisted over a period of time. Three patients with advanced pulmonary tubercolosis were evacuated immediately to the Zone of the Interior.

On 6 April the hospital was relieved from assignment to Advance Section Communications Zone and assigned to Channel Base Section Communication Zone. Also in April the personnel of the 76th mourned the passing away of President Franklin Delano Roosevelt, who had died of a cerebral haemorrhage. Tribute was paid to him at a memorial service on the post.

On 1 May a sixty day evacuation policy was instituted, replacing the previous ten day rule. This meant that patients could be treated at the hospital if they would make enough improvement to be returned to duty in 60 days thus making it unnecessary to evacuate so many patients. In the month of May no patients were admitted to the hospital. In June two other U.S. Hospitals in the area were closed and the remaining patients were transferred to the 76th. This meant that the hospital was again functioning at almost peak capacity. The 76th evacuated as many as possible to the Zone of the Interior and as patient numbers dropped wards were shut. A process using a point system was begun so that personnel from the 76th could be sent home.

In August two of the personnel from the 76th were married by the Army Chaplain. Captain Walter Menello married Nurse First Leiutenant Mary Roberson. The couple had first met on the *U.S.A.T. George Washington* on the journey to Liverpool from Boston. Capatin Menello had been injured in the hand and chest in the V1 attack that killed 25 enlisted men in January. The couple married on 11 August in Liege. Mary wore a dress she had made from silk parachute material. She had taken apart an old army uniform to make the pattern. She had hand stitched the silk into a dropped waist, scalloped neckline gown, complete with train. The couple spent their honeymoon on a trip to the French Riviera.

Soon after V.E. Day the Red Cross girls noticed a change in the patients:

"No longer is there an expression of gratitude and 'take care of the other guy, he is worse than me', especially for ambulatories ... Everywhere on the wards, in the offices there is petty thieving. It seems like a wave of lawlessness and completely lacking in recognition of another's property." (76th General Hospital Archives)

The Red Cross was kept busy with casework during this time. One unusual case was described in the narrative report for March to April. While the unit was based in Vancouver, Washington in 1944 a Pfc. with the 76th had met and, against the chaplain's advice, married a girl with a 'dubious reputation'. On the eve of the unit's departure for the P.O.E. a cable arrived at the hospital stating that the wife had been murdered and asking for burial directions. The only paperwork to be found on the body was an insurance policy belonging to the soldier. The soldier displayed little emotion on receiving the cable but sent instructions and money for the burial.

Mary Roberson and Walter Menello.

CHAPTER 6 – THE BATTLE OF GENERAL MUD

While in Liege this soldier was seen to be often accompanied by a blond Belgian girl and a little boy of about 10 or 11. One day the soldier came to tell the Commanding Officer that he had asked the girl, Sylvia, to marry him immediately. Martha Wolk, who had a good command of French, was called on to translate for the woman who couldn't speak English. The Pfc. had only a limited understanding of French.

The girl explained that her stepfather had demanded that the hospital show him a medical report stating that the soldier was free from disease and that he was healthy. As the interview continued it became obvious that the stepfather, a veteran of World War 1, was violent with an uncontrollable temper and that the soldier wanted to marry the girl immediately to remove her from the home environment. Interviews with Sylvia's mother indicated that Sylvia too had a temper and that disagreements within the family were not all caused by the stepfather.

The Commanding Officer explained the rights and privileges of wives married to American soldiers to Sylvia and there was an attempt made to explain Belgian marriage customs to the soldier. An application for permission to marry was submitted but the report doesn't record the outcome of the application.

Within the Red Cross unit there was also some friction. Around this time Martha Wolk, the A.F.D., put in a complaint about Jane Shuttleworth, the junior recreation worker and requested her removal. The Field Supervisor, Miss Evelyn Harwood, visited and interviewed the relevant parties, she reports:

"According to Miss Wolk, Miss Shuttleworth is lazy, irresponsible and furthermore has a very antagonizing attitude which has had an unfavourable effect on patients, members of the unit and the Red Cross staff. Miss Shuttleworth is described as an apparently spoiled young woman who feels no obligation to conduct herself in a courteous, more appropriate manner. She is sharp tongued, rude and inconsiderate. Furthermore she does nothing like as much work at the other members of staff, spends her time in the patient's lounge writing her own personal letters or otherwise following the dictates of her own pleasure." (76th General Hospital Archives)

When challenged Jane Shuttleworth replied that she was surprised that a complaint had been made against her and that she did not wish to leave. In her defence she stated that Martha Wolk was moody and temperamental and that she neglected her own duties, spending 90% of her time off base 'scrounging' for articles in nearby Liege, many of them not necessary for Red Cross activities.

When Dorothy Carter, the secretary, was interviewed she also stated that she found it difficult to work with Martha Wolk and reiterated Jane Shuttleworth's complaints. Dorothy objected to certain measures that Martha had taken including moving the telephone from Dorothy's desk to her own. She stated that she would like to remain at the 76th but felt that her position had become intolerable. It was left to the Field Supervisor to explain to Martha Wolk that as it was one of the secretary's duties to answer the telephone it would make sense for her to keep the phone on her desk.

Lila Wright, the Senior Recreation worker, also told the Field Supervisor that she questioned Martha Wolk's ability to lead the unit. She explained that while the main body of the unit was at Barons Cross she had been assigned to Detachment B which was sent to Northern Ireland. In Northern Ireland the two Red Cross workers had organised recreational activities efficiently and she was surprised on her return to Barons Cross that the same was not happening there. She said that at one point it had been necessary for Colonel Fancher to give Martha Wolk a deadline of a week to organise Red Cross activities and if they were not up and running by then he would close the building allotted to the Red Cross. According to Lila, Martha spent too much time on trips to the local area which did not produce anything of value to the Red Cross.

At this time Lila Wright had a skin complaint that Martha Wolk attributed to the stress of working with Jane Shuttleworth so the Field Supervisor spoke to the doctor treating her who said that it was possible that the skin complaint had been aggravated by stress but also suggested that she may be menopausal, a condition which, in his opinion, could lead to the exaggeration of problems.

Mary Newell was also interviewed. She agreed with Lila Wright's judgment of Martha Wolk but also described Jane Shuttleworth as lazy and inefficient and stated that if she was:

"an employer of Miss Shuttleworth in a business she would not tolerate her for five minutes." (76th General Hospital Archives)

When interviewed Special Services Officer, Lieutenant Kidd, who had won awards for his Special Services work with the 76th, told the Field Supervisor that he had also noticed a change in Martha Wolk's attitude. He did admit that he had requested her to procure some items off post for Special Services because she had a better command of French, stating:

CHAPTER 6 – THE BATTLE OF GENERAL MUD

"She had the time but my duties keep me busy on the post." (76th General Hospital Archives)

The Field Supervisor pointed out that Martha's duties should also keep her on the post so Lieutenant Kidd agreed not to ask her to procure items for him in the future. The Field Supervisor concluded that she needed to advise Martha Wolk to change the way she carried out her duties and she was asked to remain on the post in an attempt to discontinue her 'scrounging trips'.

"she was told that whereas Miss Shuttleworth is without a doubt a problem, at the present time the A.F.D. problem is a bigger one." (76th General Hospital Archives)

Jane Shuttleworth was given a warning and a trial period to improve her attitude.

Three weeks later Evelyn Harwood visited the post again and spoke to the Commanding Officer, Colonel Cooney. Although the Colonel had not been Commander of the 76th for long he admitted that he could see that Martha Wolk annoyed many of the personnel and that the Red Cross 'was not a happy family'. At this point the future of the 76th was uncertain, it seemed likely that it may be sent to the Pacific Theater of Operations. If it was there would be an opportunity to replace some of the Red Cross personnel so Miss Harwood decided to wait until the future was clearer to take action. A report written a month later stated that there was still no improvement in the situation.

On 27 August 1945 the hospital closed to patients and the 76th were ordered to take over the operation of the 30th General Hospital, a brick built structure in Antwerp, caring for 500 patients. Red Cross personnel were changed at this point. Mary Newell stayed with the 76th and became A.F.D. She was assigned three new Red Cross personnel to work with. At the end of September the 76th were given orders that they would be replaced by the 194th General Hospital at Antwerp and due to the victory in Japan the personnel could be sent home to be discharged.

CHAPTER 7

BRIDGING THE GAP BETWEEN THE HOSPITAL BED AND THE FOXHOLE (135TH GENERAL HOSPITAL)

The 135th General Hospital arrived at Barons Cross on 12 July and that evening took over the actively functioning hospital plant with 700 patients, from the 76th General Hospital

The 135th General Hospital had been activated on 25 May 1943 at Camp Ellis, Illinois. At this point it was known as the 269th Station Hospital. On 23 December 1943 the hospital was transferred to Fort Benning, Georgia, where it became redesignated as the 135th General Hospital. The Commanding Officer, Colonel George W. Shelton, the Executive Officer, Lieutenant Colonel Ben V. Myers and the Adjutant, Captain Edgar A. Davis led the hospital from the beginning. The Red Cross unit joined the hospital staff in May 1944 at Fort Benning.

The 135th left for the Boston Port of Embarkation on 13 June 1944 and sailed on the *U.S.S. West Point* to Gouroch, arriving on 4 July, they then entrained for the staging area in Llandudno. Nurse Claudia Cooke Kamer remembers that they were welcomed at the port in Gouroch by a bagpipe band which played 'The Star Spangled Banner'. On 12 July the unit left Llandudno for Barons Cross. The personnel soon made themselves at home in their new billets. The Special Services Officer, Lieutenant Roland Johnson remembers being assigned to hut 103 along with six other officers including the Catholic chaplain, Father John P. Condon. The men decided to name their new home 'Six Sinners

CHAPTER 7 – BRIDGING THE GAP BETWEEN THE HOSPITAL BED AND THE FOXHOLE

and a Saint' and made a wooden nameplate to hang up. The nurses also made an effort to make their quarters homely, sewing curtains and brightly coloured bed covers, some even laid out flower beds and vegetable gardens outside the huts.

The personnel had very little time to prepare themselves for running the hospital. They were immediately faced with the problems of developing an unfinished hospital plant and simultaneously dealing with the constant arrival of new patients.

The hospital was now getting a steady influx of patients arriving by train from the combat in Europe. Hospital trains with patients for the 135th arrived at Leominster Station as they did when the 76th ran the hospital. It was necessary for the 135th to develop a system for collecting patients from the station.

Upon notification by the 12th Hospital Center of an expected hospital train all the hospital personnel were alerted to participate in admitting the patients to hospital. Major Claiborne, the Receiving and Evacuation Officer, was responsible for overseeing the procedure and for providing all the relevant information. Two officers and three enlisted men were transported to Hereford, twelve miles from Leominster, to board the train early. Their duties were to examine records and assign the patients to the necessary ward. When the train arrived in Leominster each patient had a card with the ward to which he was assigned printed on it.

Upon the train's arrival at Leominster it entered a siding where around 65 men were waiting in 'litter teams' to unload the litter patients. Ambulances were driven up and patients transported to the hospital. Ambulatory patients left the train on the opposite side and were transported by bus to the hospital. There were approximately 300 patients on each train and the time required for unloading each train varied between 35 and 45 minutes.

The Medical Supply Section of the 135th had the responsibility for supplying the hospital trains which brought the patients. The train commander would forward a list of supplies needed, including rations, several hours before the train's arrival. If the train was a litter train sufficient litters to replace those removed to the hospital would be required. To save time the department would 'dress' the litters with blankets. Neatly dressed litters were placed in the train when those occupied by patients had been removed.

The ambulances containing litter patients drove to the hospital and stopped in front of the Receiving and Evacuation Office where litter teams were waiting to transport the patients to the wards. By the time the patients arrived on the ward warm meals were available and preliminary and medical care was instituted. The ambulatory patients were admitted through the Red Cross building.

Above: *Nameplate for hut 103* (R. Johnson).

Right: *Roland Johnson* (R. Johnson).

Below: *Gardens planted outside H.Q. Building* (135th General Hospital Archives).

CHAPTER 7 – BRIDGING THE GAP BETWEEN THE HOSPITAL BED AND THE FOXHOLE

In the Red Cross building the Red Cross staff met the ambulatory patients and distributed comfort articles. Some patients had been evacuated by air from the continent and had no possessions with them. The girls distributed cigarettes, matches, chewing gum, candy, stationery and soap as was required. When the litter patients had been processed in the Receiving and Evacuation Office the girls would collect their details and visit them on the ward, distributing comfort articles to them within two hours of their arrival. (To keep the patients informed the A.R.C. printed a poster giving the weekly programme of activities, which they displayed around the hospital. The first was printed on 31 July 1944.)

During the Battle of the Bulge a large number of patients were admitted and the hospital became full to capacity. Roland Johnson remembers that at one point 2000 beds were needed for patients. Up to this point the 135th had continued the system commenced by the 76th, using some of the Medical Service wards for the Surgical Service as the hospital was still primarily an orthopaedic hospital. However during the Battle of the Bulge a large number of patients were received who needed medical treatment for trench foot and at this point it was necessary to transfer some wards back to the Medical Service.

As spring started to arrive, the weather conditions in France started to improve. Less trench foot patients were received and it was necessary to change the ward organisation back. The majority of patients received from February 1945 needed surgical treatment with orthopaedic work dominating. 75% of convoys received in March and April were made up of patients needing orthopaedic work. 960 patients were treated from January to May 1945 by the orthopaedic section. It was also noticed that patients received from January to May 1945 had worse injuries than those received in the six months previously and a number of them had severe abdominal injuries.

On arrival at the hospital it was necessary to work to a system to treat the orthopaedic patients according to need so a system was set up. Emergency cases were treated immediately, then amputation cases. All other cases were treated as early as possible to avoid leaving patients in dirty casts fitted while in evacuation hospitals. The average convoy was seen in the operating room within five to seven days after arrival for the first change of cast, inspection of wounds and early closure of wounds where feasible.

Orthopaedic personnel were put into teams of two or three medical officers with enlisted men to assist. One team would work in the operating room in the morning and one in the afternoon. This system enabled officers to follow up their patient's progress on the wards when they were not in the operating theatre. Each officer

Wards (135th General Hospital Archives).

View of ward area (135th General Hospital Archives).

CHAPTER 7 – BRIDGING THE GAP BETWEEN THE HOSPITAL BED AND THE FOXHOLE

was assigned a variety of different cases in the operating room so that he became proficient at a number of different procedures such as inserting kirschener wires for suspended traction, applying casts of all kinds, performing secondary closure wounds, removing foreign bodies and carrying out re-amputation.

Following the operation the patient was taken to the appropriate ward unless convalescence ward care was required because of anaesthesia or a complicating factor such as haemorrhage or shock. The hospital organised the orthopaedic wards so that each ward cared for a specific injury: damage to femurs, humeri, tibias, forearms, amputation cases and miscellaneous fractures. The orthopaedic department believed that grouping together patients with similar injuries helped with morale. When a large convoy of 200 to 300 was admitted, due to the scarcity of beds it was not always possible to send patients to the specific ward for their injury straight away but staff endeavoured to send them to the correct ward after being operated on.

Traction cases were taken to their ward by a 'pin up' team and immediately placed in balanced traction. X-rays were taken on all traction cases within the first 24 hours so that progress could be monitored.

Enlisted personnel in the Orthopaedic section were trained in the preparation of plaster of paris rolls, the technique of applying various types of casts and splints and setting up balanced traction. Part of the clinic was devoted to the preparation of plaster rolls of various sizes. The plaster rolling was carried out by hand on a machine designed for the purpose. Enough rolls were prepared for the theatre and clinic and the exact number of rolls necessary for an individual type of case was computed to avoid waste. During the period January to July 1945 over one and a half tons of plaster was used by the orthopaedic section. The enlisted men assisted the Medical Officers in applying casts. Stress was laid on the importance of having a smooth application of plaster and Lieutenant Colonel Parker, Chief of the surgical service noted that:

"Each enlisted man took pride in the finished product." (135th General Hospital Archives)

In amputation cases it was found inconvenient to change dressings of a stump with the cast on so a removable shell cast was devised using a piece of web strapping with a buckle on the end incorporated into the cast. The entire cast could then be removed and replaced at will. This had the added advantage that the cast could be loosened or tightened as the occasion demanded.

From January to July 1945 there were three deaths on the Surgical Service. One occurred less than 12 hours after admission. A British Glider Flight Officer was admitted with a compound fracture of the skull along with a fracture of the cervical vertebrae. The second case died within 36 hours from a haemorrhage. The third patient had been admitted from the 107th General Hospital when it closed. He died five days after admission from multiple fistulae and abscesses.

The Medical Service treated patients on medical wards. Between February and April 1945 a large number of cases of jaundice were admitted. The men suffering from jaundice were put on a high carbohydrate, high protein low fat diet and vitamin therapy. All recovered and returned to duty. In May 1945 when evacuation to the Zone of the Interior was mandatory after sixty days of hospitalisation it was necessary to board to the Zone of the Interior some patients who needed a longer course of treatment for jaundice. Eight soldiers from German captivity who had severe malnutrition were admitted to the 135th in May. All responded well to treatment, each of them gaining a pound a day during their 33 day hospitalisation.

From January to July 1945 315 neuro-psychiatric casualties were admitted to the Medical Service. In contrast with patients admitted in the first few months following D-Day these patients had all been hospitalised for a minimum of four to six weeks prior to admission to the 135th. For many of these casualties the admission was the second or third for the same difficulties. Many had been treated for 'combat exhaustion' and been placed on limited assignment only to have their symptoms return.

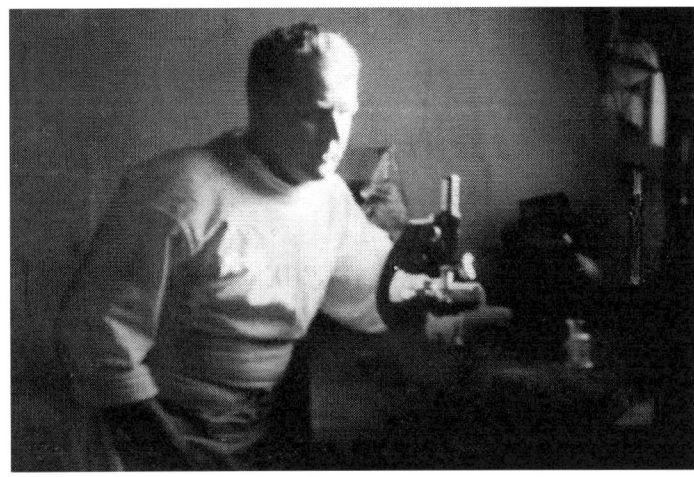

View of inside of laboratory (135th General Hospital Archives).

CHAPTER 7 – BRIDGING THE GAP BETWEEN THE HOSPITAL BED AND THE FOXHOLE

Because of the limited bed space and the severity of their symptoms it was necessary to return a large number of these patients to the Zone of the Interior for intensive treatment that could be carried out for as long as each individual patient needed. During their stay in hospital the patients received group therapy and were placed in a rehabilitation programme organised and administered by the Neuropsychiatric Section. Infantry officers who had been hospitalised as psychiatric casualties were utilised throughout the programme. This programme helped to keep patients out of beds and off the wards.

Once patients in the surgical and medical wards had completed their treatment they were sent to the Zone of Interior if their condition would prevent them from returning to duty. If they were to return to duty they would take part in the Rehabilitation Programme.

"The mission of the Rehabilitation Programme of the 135th General Hospital was to prepare hospitalized men, physically and mentally, for return to combat duty. Its purpose was to bridge the gap between the hospital bed and the foxhole." (135th General Hospital Archives)

Ward officers would transfer patients to the Rehabilitation Section when their condition had improved sufficiently to permit them to engage in the training programme. On admission to the section the trainee was examined by the Rehabilitation Medical officer and graded according to his physical condition into Class A or B. A note was made of any remedial exercises that might be needed, his wounds examined and the nature of his illness or injury checked against the diagrams on the chart. In some instances further investigations into a man's physical or mental condition were needed before rehabilitation could begin.

Following the patient's admission to the Rehabilitation Section he was considered to be a 'Rehabilitation Trainee' rather than a 'Hospital Patient', his convalescent suit was discarded and replaced by a set of fatigues. During the graded training programme of two weeks the trainee would take part in calisthenics, road marches and attend lectures. The lectures consisted of orientation talks and training talks on subjects such as map reading, first aid and weapons. After two weeks the patient's case was reviewed by the Medical Officer of the Rehabilitation Section and his disposition decided.

Patients who were not ready for full rehabilitation would fall into Classes C and D. Patients in Class C were given one hour physical training in the gymnasium and three hours occupational therapy in the Red Cross workshop daily. Bed patients (Class D) were given 15 minutes bed exercise twice daily by the Physical Director over the P.A. system. Occupational therapy for this group was given by the Red Cross staff. Remedial physiotherapy was given to Class D patients on the ward as directed by the ward officer.

The last hospital train was received at the 135th General Hospital on 9 May, the day after V.E. Day. Many of the wounded of this convoy had seen action in Czechoslovakia and Austria and were received in the hospital 72 – 96 hours after being wounded. In June the bed status of the hospital was reduced to 750 and on 6 July the 135th General Hospital ceased functioning as a hospital. All personnel were put under redeployment orders for possible redeployment to the Pacific Theater of Operations.

CHAPTER 8

MEDICALLY APPROVED INDIVIDUAL AND GROUP RECREATION (135ᵀᴴ GENERAL HOSPITAL)

Religious welfare at the 135th was taken care of by the two chaplains. Father Condon, the Catholic chaplain, organised services and events for the Catholics on base and even conducted weddings at the Catholic Church in Leominster when called upon. The Protestant chaplain, Captain Prince Turner lists his activities while at the 135th. His duties included: …

> *"… daily ward visits, occasional emergency calls, regular chapel services, letters of condolence for seriously ill patients, sharing the burden of bad news from the loved ones at home with patients and detachment personnel, recreational and educational tours, office training programmes, civilian community activity, chaplains conferences and a week at Divinity school at Edinburgh University."* (135 General Hospital Archives)

A district Jewish chaplain catered for those of the Jewish faith at the hospital and Pastor Howard from London met with Seventh Day Adventist personnel at regular quarterly intervals.

The personnel from the base also attended local churches such as the Moravian Mission church in Cholstrey. When Barons Cross camp closed down a number of army service hymnals were donated to the church.

Above: *Interior of Base chapel* (135th General Hospital Archives).

Left: *Inside view of the Detachment Day Room* (135th General Hospital Archives).

CHAPTER 8 – MEDICALLY APPROVED INDIVIDUAL AND GROUP RECREATION

Recreational and Educational activities for the staff and patients of the 135th were jointly organised by Special Services and the Red Cross. Lieutenant Roland Johnson led the Special Services. He organised sporting activities such as the intramural basketball and softball programmes. He also made arrangements for the men to use the local facilities such as golf courses, tennis courts and swimming pools. In cooperation with the Area Engineer a basketball court was set up by converting a storage warehouse and mess hall in Leominster.

A Detachment Day Room was furnished and a Recreational Room was served to use as a theatre. U.S.O. shows were presented here and movies were shown daily for patients and staff. Prior to obtaining this building it was necessary to show movies in the Red Cross Recreational Hall. This meant that Red Cross staff were constantly clearing away their activities and setting up the room for movies and then having to set up their activities again the next day.

Roland states that the best part of his job was to:

"bring in, supervise and partake of all the outside entertainment that was available to us. This meant shows of all kinds for both the personnel at the hospital and all the patients."

The A.R.C. unit at the 135th carried out a number of roles in the hospital from meeting convoys of patients when they first arrived at the hospital to catering for all their recreational needs while they were there. They also organised recreational activities for the detachment personnel.

The A.R.C. unit at Barons Cross consisted of 5 workers and a British civilian secretary. They were also assigned two British civilian maids and a full time detachment man to run the public address system as a miniature broadcasting station.

When the P.A. system was installed in November 1944 a special studio was built for the broadcasting station in one of the Red Cross buildings. The corporal assigned to run the station had previous broadcasting experience. Station R-E-D-X offered a continuous programme from nine in the morning till nine at night. Radio programmes were selected to be broadcast that would meet the patients' interests. The corporal also ran a regular sports programme which was hosted by one of the patients when he was on furlough. Any patients that were musically talented would be invited to the studio to play so that it could be broadcast to the patients. There was a regular slot called *'The Purple Heart Hour'*. This was an hour dedicated to the recipients of Purple Heart medals at the hospital. They would be mentioned by name and have records dedicated to them. Another programme of interest was *'Home Town Hour'* when ambulatory patients from a given town would gather together for an informal and lively half hour of talking about things from their home town. This then led to reunions with other patients who had heard the broadcast and also came from that town.

The P.A. system was used extensively in the recreation programme of the Red Cross. The girls broadcast a quiz called *'This One is Easy'* introduced by the signature tune *'I know that you know!'* Quiz teams were organised to take part in the competitions which took place in the studio. The teams were usually made up of patients but detachment personnel sometimes joined in and visiting relatives and friends occasionally made up a quiz team. Patients listening to the quiz on the P.A. system would often see if they could answer the questions too. All stage shows were broadcast to bed patients, informal interviews often took place while waiting for the show to begin.

The British Red Cross continued to send in a group of volunteer ladies to mend clothes for both patients and detachment personnel as they had when the 76th ran the hospital. The hospital had a policy of not allowing volunteer workers on the wards unaccompanied for security reasons. It was thought that patients newly arrived from combat on the continent might speak too freely about their experiences and information might get into the wrong hands.

One civilian volunteer was taken on to work as an assistant in the Recreation Hall. However it was observed that she devoted only part of her time to the Recreation Hall and the rest to the library. After the first two weeks she spent all her time in the library as she: ...

> *"... didn't care for the type of work nor the noise of the Recreational Hall."* (135th General Hospital Archives)

Another volunteer came to the hospital twice a week to teach French lessons and to talk to French speaking patients. Two other men, one a former mayor, and the other a local banker, shared the responsibility each week for an evening of card games in the Recreation Hall. A volunteer, who already had an actively functioning British military hospital on her estate, came to Barons Cross to teach crafts and donated a considerable variety of sample toys and patterns. (Presumably this was Lady Cawley of Berrington Hall)

CHAPTER 8 – MEDICALLY APPROVED INDIVIDUAL AND GROUP RECREATION

Pocket Editions of books (Author's Collection).

The Red Cross had the use of two buildings, one building was a Recreation Hall for handicrafts and the other contained a large lounge with ping pong and a snooker table; a small lounge with book shelves, writing tables and a library; a small lounge for officer patients and two small offices for interviews and group meetings. The building also contained the studio for Station R-E-D-X, a combination kitchen, store and washroom.

The library started with 800 books left by the Red Cross unit of the 76th and ended with 6,000. Many townspeople donated books to the hospital as did the hospital personnel. The girls were also able to obtain a small number of 'Pocket Editions' of novels from Red Cross Headquarters. In the library the girls stored 'scrap books' made of articles found in magazines that the patients might find interesting or useful. One was kept on the amputation ward which contained information that might help amputees e.g. prosthetic devices, vocational training, job opportunities and several accounts written by the amputees themselves.

Because of the lack of help in the Recreation Hall it was necessary for one of the two workers to be there most of the time. The other worker would then be free to cover the wards. The two Recreation Workers divided the wards between them and divided their time between the Recreation Hall and their allocated wards.

The Red Cross orientated their overall programme:

"to provide not only relief from boredom but to give constructive outlets for as much activity, ingenuity, group participation and healthy competition as each patient is capable at the various stages at his hospitalisation because we believe that the patient who is spontaneously interested in what is going on in the ward around him, and who is gaining healthy satisfaction from what he is doing is the patient whose recovery is most naturally accelerated." (135th General Hospital Archives)

The girls based their planning on the statement in the Army Regulations stating the functions of the Red Cross:

"To plan and direct medically approved individual and group recreation for bed patients and convalescents." (135th General Hospital Archives)

Due to the rapid turnover of patient personnel it was necessary to adapt the programme to meet patients' needs both for bed patients and convalescent patients who could not leave the hospital and another for rehabilitation patients who were allowed passes.

The craft programme run by the girls could be participated in by all patients. Activities were carried on in the Recreation Hall and also on the wards. The A.F.D. comments:

"With so many things to be done and so few people the value of leaving with the patient something to occupy him when the workers have left the ward speaks for itself." (135th General Hospital Archives)

She also noticed that:

"Pleasure was derived not only from the action of 'doing' but in the feeling of accomplishment – the knowledge that a patient could send Mom, Mary or Junior something that he, himself had made." (135th General Hospital Archives)

CHAPTER 8 – MEDICALLY APPROVED INDIVIDUAL AND GROUP RECREATION

As well as craft items made for loved ones a number of ambulatory patients developed equipment for other patients to use. Writing boards, frames, sloping tables and cigarette holders for those with badly burnt hands were amongst some of the items made.

After the second week of operation at the 135th arrangements were made in cooperation with local volunteers, for groups of patients to visit private homes on Sunday afternoons for high tea. Usually about twenty patients were invited each Sunday, two to four to a home. Transport was provided by the military and the visits lasted three to four hours. It was necessary to discontinue this activity in September 1944 when a new pass policy became effective. However from March 1945 it was possible again to accept the hospitality of the hospital's neighbours.

Early in September 1944 one of the volunteers was instrumental in organising trips to two of the neighbouring towns. On alternative Mondays two buses, accommodating 62 patients were loaded at 1400 hours. After a tour of places of interest in the appointed town the patients became guests of a volunteer organisation for high tea. Each group was accompanied by a volunteer worker and an officer.

In the spring 1945, through cooperation with Special Services, weekly trips to attend a matinee became a popular past time. The hospital supplied the transportation and each trip had an officer patient or staff in charge. The Rehabilitation patients were the ones to benefit from activities of this nature as the majority of the other patients were not allowed passes.

Dances were arranged in the Recreation Building for those without passes. The unit dance band, 'The 135th Woodchoppers', played at the dances. Several of the patients played as part of the detachment orchestra during their stay in hospital which was both of benefit to the orchestra and to the men themselves. Groups of girls from the land army hostel at nearby Bircher Hall and also WAAFS were invited to the dances. The Red Cross also organised small parties and dances in Leominster.

Another popular activity organised by the Red Cross was *'Baby Picture'* contests. Patients submitted pictures of their sons, daughters, nieces and nephews and they were judged by a doctor, nurse and three detachment men. Ribbons were awarded for the first four pictures. Prizes were sent home and some mothers wrote back to the Red Cross thanking them for the prize. The contest was so popular that it was repeated when there was a turnover of patients. The girls also ran a *'Big Baby'* contest, this time requiring pictures of wives, sweethearts and sisters. Along with the judge's decision there was a patient vote for *'Miss 135th'*. The detachment men were very interested in this contest so the girls ran one for personnel.

Little and Big Baby Winners in Red Cross Contests
Judges Knee Deep In Photos

Winners of the 3 baby photo contests held at the Red Cross this month are: Novaco, Champ Detachment Baby; Master, Champ Patient Baby; and Rocco, Champ Patient Big-Baby.

Runners up to Anthony Novaco in the Detachment contest were Lillian Buckley and Ronald Louise Bezy in that order. Boy prize winners up to one year were Kilby, Barrett, and Alvarado. Girl prize winners up to one year were Buckley, Pippin (niece of Sgt Nadig), and Roberts (niece of Sgt Hamill). Boys one to three: 1-Novaco, 2-Woodward (Pvt Young), 3-Como. Age three to five: 1-Bezy, 2-Taylor, 3-Barrett.

Patients Little-Baby contest champs were: 1-Kenneth Master B-3, 2-Rexwood Rexroad A-10, 3-Jean Kohler D-1. Under one year: 1-Master, 2-Wood B-3, 3-Berghbolz A-9. Girls one to three: 1-Campbell A-10, 2-Paul -1, 3-Hardy C-7. Boys one to three: 1-Cosnick B-5, 2-Cass A-2, 3-Fox A-2. Girls three to five: 1-Jean A-10, 2-Kuntz D-1, 3-Colman A-5. Three to five: 1-Poe A-1, 2-Fuchs D-2, 3-Morgan D-2.

Big-Baby champs were: 1-Rocca A-8, 2-Green C-5, 3-Bell A-5T. Prettiest girl: 1-Saylor A-3, 2-Green C-5, 3-Shaefer A-5T. Typical All-American girl: 1-Schaefer A-5T, 2-House B-4, 3-Harman A-5T.

Judges for Detachment Baby contest were Lt Col Parker, Lt Watson and patient Pvt Rexroad. Judges for Patient Little Baby contest were Chaplain Turner, Lt Koski and M Sgt Epperson. Champ Patient Big-Baby was chosen by a patient Gallup Poll. Judges in the Prettiest and Typical All-American Girl divisions were Lt Col Parker, Majors Eckstein and Jacobsen, and Sgts Engel and Gorsuch.

Baby contest as advertised in Red Cross flyer (135th General Hospital Archives).

CHAPTER 8 – MEDICALLY APPROVED INDIVIDUAL AND GROUP RECREATION

Because so many of the patients knew that casualty reports would soon be reaching their homes they were anxious to reassure their families that they were alright. The Red Cross decided to set up a photographic studio, arranging with a detachment man whose hobby was photography to have a 'photograph salon' one evening a week. For one shilling and six pence he produced three snapshots, sometimes visiting relatives were photographed with the patients. One mother wrote an especially poignant letter to the Red Cross requesting more prints of a photograph that had been sent to her. During his furlough her elder son, who was in the Air Force and whom she had not seen in three years, arranged to visit his younger brother at the 135th where the younger brother was a patient. Within 48 hours of that visit the older brother had been lost on his final mission when his plane crashed.

Social case work was an important part of the work carried out by the Red Cross at Barons Cross. Because patients were only at the hospital for a short time the social worker attempted to deal with social work of a 'short contact' nature with the exception of service given to a comparatively small number of patients who remained at the hospital over a period of some months.

The case work was wide and varied. Most of the cases involved the patients' families. There were a number of requests for the Red Cross to help locate relatives in the service. This was difficult as many military units constantly moved from one place to the other. A number of the patients had marriage problems, often they were upset because a neighbour or family member had written to tell them that their wives had been unfaithful or were even pregnant. Some patients had enjoyed the freedom that they had away from the marital home so much that they did not want to return to it. Other patients just wanted to sit in a quiet office and share with someone their feelings over the loss of someone close to them. Some patients needed help to accept their physical handicaps and a special project was undertaken to work with amputees at the hospital.

One paratrooper, who had been informed of the serious illness of his three year old child, sought assistance from the Red Cross. The paratrooper had two children, the older one was cared for by his mother and the younger by his estranged wife. The patient blamed his wife for the younger child's illness and threatened to go A.W.O.L. when he heard that his application for emergency furlough had been refused because of the policy at the time. The social worker tried to help him by talking through his worries and making constructive plans for his future. The Red Cross were able to ask a former lawyer in the detachment to give the man information about changes in divorce laws in the serviceman's home state and a

Left: *Photo of George Seiffart, Father Condon, Roland Johnson, Don McIntyre* (R. Johnson).

Below: *Christmas choir practising in Base Chapel* (135th General Hospital Archives).

CHAPTER 8 – MEDICALLY APPROVED INDIVIDUAL AND GROUP RECREATION

referral was made to a child placing agency which could arrange the temporary care of his daughter. News of the daughter's steady improvement was a help to the man's state of mind as was the news that the extent of his injuries meant that he would be soon sent home.

At Christmas 1944 the Red Cross were particularly busy. Posters announcing the 'Best Decorated Ward' contest were put up early in December. Basic decorating supplies were allocated to each ward and ward doctors, nurses and patients set to work. Trees were donated by local people and put in containers for every ward in the hospital with large ones for the day rooms and mess halls. The local electric company volunteered to supply the tree with coloured lights. The judges made their rounds on Christmas Eve afternoon and the results were announced that evening over the P.A. system.

The three mess kitchens started baking each night for the Red Cross and eventually produced around 14,000 cookies. The sewing volunteers helped to wrap the packages and fill the 1600 stockings. Christmas cards were printed in Leominster and were enclosed with the packages. The girls managed to produce two packages and a stocking for every patient and detachment man. They planned to tie the stockings to the beds on Christmas Eve late at night but had to change their plans when they discovered that a convoy of patients were due to arrive at 0400 Christmas morning.

Several programmes were scheduled for the Christmas period. The Protestant and Catholic choirs broadcast carols on the P.A. system. On the Friday before Christmas a group of 40 children from the local school put on a programme in the Recreation Hall which was broadcast to all the wards. After this, part of the group visited some of the wards to sing. Previous to this the children had visited and sung to some of the servicemen billeted in the town.

As the programme finished in the Recreation Hall the detachment party was held in the other Red Cross building complete with Santa Claus, the distribution of parcels, singing and entertainment. On Saturday night the officers' party was held where one of the doctors acted as Santa Claus.

A couple of days before Christmas Major Fay, the Commanding Officer of one of the American units in town, wrote an article for the Leominster Journal thanking the people of the town for their kindness to the personnel and patients of the hospital. He expressed the wish that as a result of the people of Leominster coming to know 'The Yank': ...

"... both John Bull and Uncle Sam can better fit themselves to work side by side towards our common objective: a world of peace, justice and love to be shared by all men at good will." (Leominster Journal, 23/2/1944)

He also wished the people of the town a Merry Christmas and a Victorious New Year.

On Christmas Eve a Christmas programme was presented by several patients, detachment men, Red Cross workers, Officers and the two choirs. Afterwards there was a period of group carolling. The patient party was held after this.

On Christmas morning the Red Cross split into two groups each with a Santa. (One Santa was a detachment man and the other a local citizen) It took the entire morning to cover the hospital as each patient was individually greeted by Santa as the gift packages and stockings were distributed. Even the patients that had arrived that morning were included. On the last ward the two Santas met, which caused some amusement to the patients.

American Red Cross Staff receiving presents off Santa (135th General Hospital Archives).

CHAPTER 8 – MEDICALLY APPROVED INDIVIDUAL AND GROUP RECREATION

Christmas afternoon at the 135th was fairly quiet as most of the hospital had been kept awake until the early hours by the arrival of the convoy. That evening another programme was held for the patients. The A.F.D. reports:

"The comments were received personally and in letters afterwards indicated that we had succeeded in helping to ease a time when home sickness and sadness were not far below the surface and to make a home like 'good fellowship' feeling pervade as much as possible." (135th General Hospital Archives)

In May 1945 another celebration was planned at the 135th, this time it was the anniversary of the birth of the 269th Station Hospital that had formed the core of the 135th. The party was held at the Detachment Mess Hall with a dinner which featured music, speeches, steak, ice-cream, cake and gifts. The members of the original cadre sat at the head table with the Detachment Commander.

When the operations of the 135th were finished in July 1945 the Red Cross A.F.D. summed up her feelings about the year spent in Leominster.

"In summarising our feelings at the close of this phase of operation, I think it can truthfully be said we tried to do what we could within our capabilities and limitations, to make life more enjoyable for the patients during their stay here, and to help in any way possible towards the preparation of themselves for their return to home or duty." (135th General Hospital Archives)

CHAPTER 9

TWO ALLIED FRIENDLY NATIONS (135TH GENERAL HOSPITAL)

Over the year that the 135th served at Barons Cross there were some changes to the personnel. Because of the heavy losses in the Battle of the Bulge in early 1945 the hospital was required to send enlisted personnel who were surplus to the hospital's efficient running to the Reinforcement system for infantry conversion training. Some limited assignment and ex-combat personnel were furnished as basic replacements.

Some of the more menial jobs at the hospital could be taken on by the German P.O.W.s assigned to the hospital. A P.O.W. camp consisting of huts and tentage for 150 P.O.W.s was erected adjacent to the hospital by the engineers. The P.O.W.s were utilised in various detail duties in kitchens, ground police and maintenance and were held under the jurisdiction of the Labor Provincial Company consisting of one officer and three enlisted men. A detachment of a further 30 enlisted men were trained in firearms and used as perimeter and detail guards for the P.O.W. camp. The camp was closed on 7 July 1945.

A Fire Protection and Control section was maintained at the 135th. One officer was appointed Fire Marshall and four more were appointed assistants, each having a fire zone to police. The men had the use of a modified ¾ ton weapons carrier with a Coventry trailer pump to use for fire fighting. The vehicle was maintained by the Motor Pool. A regular fire detail of eight enlisted men was maintained, four of

CHAPTER 9 – TWO ALLIED FRIENDLY NATIONS

Main gate (135th General Hospital Archives).

whom were on duty at one time. Regular fire drills were held monthly. Two minor fires occurred during 1945, both caused by sparks from stoves getting under roof-jacks and smouldering. These fires were extinguished immediately with very little damage sustained.

Other accidents involving vehicles from the hospital were investigated, all were of a minor nature and only in one case were minor personal injuries sustained, when a civilian cyclist suffered a sprained ankle. In none of the accidents were the drivers found responsible.

The 135th also had a Military Police and Guard detachment of approximately 18 men under the command of the Provost Marshall, Captain William Jones. The M.P. detachment was required for policing the hospital plant and also for coordinating with the civilian police in Leominster to police the town. The unit operated the main gatepost and checked all military and civilian personnel and vehicles entering or leaving the post. It also furnished guards for all U.S.O. shows and movies. The functions of the M.P. detachment were:

View from the main gate (135th General Hospital Archives).

1. To maintain discipline of all military personnel both on and off the post in regard to military courtesy, uniform violations and proper conduct in nearby towns.

2. To check local Public houses and railway stations checking for pass violations, apprehending A.W.O.Ls and returning them to their units.

3. To cooperate with civilian police in instances involving U.S. personnel.

4. To control traffic in the local area when convoy movements were scheduled.

5. To maintain Post Guardhouses with three eight-hour shifts.

6. To maintain records and forward reports.

The Leominster Journal records a number of incidents involving U.S. soldiers and local people in drunken brawls where it was necessary for the M.P.s to become involved.

In June 1944 four youths were charged with assaulting three American soldiers and in the process damaging a pair of spectacles, in a fight that started outside the Black Swan. In a statement the American soldiers stated that the British youths had

CHAPTER 9 – TWO ALLIED FRIENDLY NATIONS

started the fight and they were merely fighting in self-defence. One of the British youths was chased by an M.P. and alleged that he was hit with a truncheon although there were no witnesses to this. For the assault one youth received a month's imprisonment and three others were fined. The magistrate commented that:

> *"We take a very serious view of those cases. It is disgraceful to think that these men, our American allies, who have come over here and who are given a hearty welcome by the general public should be set upon and assaulted by a party of Leominster hooligans."* (Leominster Journal 2/6/44)

In February 1945 there was a similar case when American officer, Franklin Clarke, (a patient from Barons Cross who was recovering from an operation) was assaulted by a British sailor, Albert Hacket and his younger brother.

The American officer was returning home from a dance accompanied by a girl when he heard a voice asking: "Are you a Yank?" When he stopped a sailor came over to him and punched him in the jaw, he hit a wall and fell to the ground where the sailor kicked him several times. The girl tried to help but she too was hit. She ran across the road to ask Private John Rogers to help, he arrived and was hit also.

Meanwhile the sailor's younger brother, Leslie, had gone up to another American officer, 2nd Lieutenant Di Luvio and asked him for a light. As he lifted his arm to give him a light from his cigarette Leslie Hacket hit him. The M.P.s arrived and the two Leominster men lashed out at them too. Casper Ivey stated that the sailor:

> *"...let me have a couple and I got out of his way."*

Albert Hacket's defence was that:

> *"Clarke's blow would have been very slight had it not been for the icy conditions of the road. The blow was struck in self-defence."* (Leominster Journal 16/2/45)

Leslie Hacket said that he had accidently knocked into the American who had used a *'term of abuse'* to him which he did not regard lightly and that is why he hit him.

There were several witnesses who had seen the two British men punching, kicking and swearing at the American servicemen. One lady had seen the sailor taking a running kick at the American and heard him say:

"If any of the American Army want to fight bring them down to me and I will fight them." (Leominster Journal 16/2/45)

Both of the Hackets were charged with assaulting 2nd Lieutenant Di Luvio and Albert Hacket was charged with assaulting Private Rogers and Private Casper M. Ivey and for assaulting Franklin Clarke and causing bodily harm. (Clarke received head injuries and was kept in hospital) Both men received fines.

Mr Wallis, speaking for the defence: ...

"... expressed regret that any such conflict as this should have arisen between the two Allied services engaged in the same good cause and two Allied friendly nations, more particularly since those concerned in the prosecution were honoured guests in the country." (Leominster Journal 16/2/45)

Other less violent crimes involving U.S. servicemen were reported in the Leominster Journal. In April 1945 a 15 year old gypsy was arrested for stealing instruments from the Lyonshall Memorial Hall after an American dance band had played there. At first he denied the charges but then admitted that he and another boy had climbed through the open window of the hall, drunk some beer out of bottles that had been left there and took the instruments. The boy was able to show the Police Sergeant where he had hidden the instruments in a hedge and return them so the bench decided to discharge the boy under the 'Probation of Offences Act'!

Another case reported in the Leominster Journal tells of a girl who was under 16 being charged for 'sleeping out'. She was found in an air raid shelter with two American servicemen. She said that she had met one of the soldiers at a dance and had slept with him because he had forced her into the shelter where she later fell asleep. The soldier and the girl were found underneath a number of army blankets while another serviceman was sitting on the bench. The door to the shelter had been wedged shut with a stone on the inside. When the mother of the girl was interviewed she said that:

"She was quite out of control and took no notice of what was said to her!" (Leominster Journal 16/3/45)

The school attendance officer reiterated the fact that there was 'a complete lack of parental control'. It was thought that because no parent was exercising proper care over

CHAPTER 9 – TWO ALLIED FRIENDLY NATIONS

her 'she was exposed to moral danger'. (Leominster Journal 16/3/45) Because of this and the fact that it was not the first time the police had warned her about her behaviour she was sent to an approved school for which her parents had to pay 7s 6d per week.

Fortunately there were accounts of happier unions between the British and the Americans which were reported in the Leominster Journal. On 25 February the wedding of Ivy Porter from Essex and T/5 Milton Hall of Vincennes, Indiana, took place at Leominster Priory Church. PFC Andrew Wood of New Jersey was best man and the bride was given away by another American serviceman, Staff Sergeant Jay T. Shannon of Kansas City. The couple spent their honeymoon in London.

The following month one of the nurses at the 135th Lieutenant Mary Virginia Crowley, married 1st Sergeant James R. Lowe, an American paratrooper, at Leominster Roman Catholic Church. Lieutenant Margie Englert, a friend of the bride, was bridesmaid. Father Condon officiated at the wedding.

The Americans also enjoyed good relationships with the children of the town. This could have been partly because of the G.I.s' generosity with sweets and gum. Pauline Davies remembers the G.I.s giving her a type of red gum called soap doap, which she didn't particularly like. Colin Beard remembers the occasion that a military vehicle broke down outside his house. His parents took out some refreshments for the crew and the driver gave Colin some gum. John Whittall remembers that his mother used to take in washing for the servicemen at Barons Cross. He remembers going to the camp, collecting washing for his mother, gum for himself and his sister and cigarettes for his father.

Priory Church, Leominster May 1944 (Olavi Oja).

Good relationships between the British and Americans were cemented with the post V.E. Day party organised by the Americans for the children at Leominster. On V.E. Day, which was a public holiday, the town council had organised very little in the way of events as:

"In the manner of general celebrations it was felt that in view of the fact that the war against Japan was not yet over and that there would be many heavy hearts that day that nothing official should be arranged, that each person should spend the day as he pleased!" (Leominster Journal)

It was suggested that a cricket match should take place but it was pointed out that the pitch was not ready and there was not enough time to get it ready. It was also suggested that the band could play in the square but it was pointed out that many of the bandsmen were away in the services. Finally the Council decided on a thanksgiving service at the Priory Church. There were also two dances in the evening. Some streets, like Mill Street, organised their own street parties.

On 23 May an invitation for the children of Leominster to attend a party on the 25th was put in the Leominster Journal by the Red Cross. All children between the ages of five and fourteen were invited and it was estimated that around 1,000 children took up the invitation.

 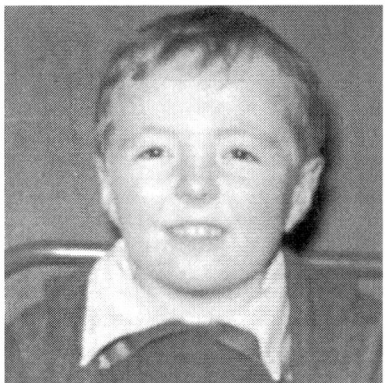

Above left: *Marriage of Mary Crowley and James Lowe* (Leominster Journal 6/4/45).

Above right: *John Whittall* (S. Whittall).

CHAPTER 9 – TWO ALLIED FRIENDLY NATIONS

> **LEOMINSTER CHILDREN TO CELEBRATE**
> **NEXT WEEK'S ENTERTAINMENT BY AMERICANS**
>
> To the Editor of the Leominster News.
>
> Sir,—In grateful appreciation of all the many kindnesses extended to the patients and staff of the local American Military Hospital, we, the undersigned, with the freely given co-operation of the directors and staff of the Clifton Cinema, are authorised to invite all the Leominster children between the ages of 5 and 14 to attend a Victory Celebration on Wednesday next, May 23rd. The children will assemble at their respective schools at 1.30 p.m. and will be escorted to a special children's performance at the Cinema. Following this there will be tea and music at the Friends' Meeting house, across the street from the Cinema, to which all children from five to fourteen are invited
>
> Yours, etc.,
> For the Commanding Officer, American Hospital,
> PRINCE E. TURNER,
> (Capt.) Ch.C., A.U.S.
> MARGUERITE V. POHEK,
> Assistant Field Director, American Red Cross.
> E. WINN,
> MARY PAGE,
> Local Organisers.

Leominster Journal 18/5/45.

A committee, which included the Red Cross Girls, the Protestant chaplain, Captain Prince Turner, the cinema manager, a landowner (Mr Bateman) and a civilian volunteer, worked together to formulate the plans for the occasion. Mr Bateman arranged the use of the New Exchange Building for the refreshments.

At 1.30pm the Boys Brigade Band paraded from the junior school heading a procession of children, marshalled by several Americans, to the Clifton Cinema. The band then marched to the senior school and escorted the children from there to the cinema. British and American flags flew side by side in the procession. At the cinema the children watched a programme of films and then the chaplain said a few words of appreciation to the people of the town for what they had done for the servicemen during their time in Leominster.

At 4.00pm the children were lined up this time to march to the New Exchange Building. This had been set out with tables and benches and decorated with decorations designed and made by the patients at Barons Cross. The children were served cocoa, tea or milk and helped themselves to sandwiches and cakes. One of the girls at the party remembers that one of the boys bypassed the sandwiches and started on the cakes straight away. She remembers that he ate all the fancy tops off all the cakes and left the plain bases for the rest of the children on his table. Pauline Davis remembers that some of the children went to Barons Cross for their refreshments. She recalls eating gateau there made by a chef she called 'Blue Eyes'.

While they ate the Detachment Orchestra 'The 135th Woodchoppers' played for the children. The Red Cross secretary notes in the archives:

Leominster Journal (25/5/45).

G.I.s marshalling the children (M. Mason).

CHAPTER 9 – TWO ALLIED FRIENDLY NATIONS

"It was something to hear the din and excitement of a thousand children and it was hard to determine which of the groups – the adults or the children – were having the most fun. At the end of the hour filled with song, music, laughter and even a few tears – there were the inevitable broken or overturned mugs – the party came to a close. As each child left he was given two candy bars and gum collected from the detachment and officers of the entire outfit, and a three penny bit and several magazines, including comics. The comments from the children and parents alike indicated that the day would long remain in their memory." (135th General Hospital Archives)

After the party the Chaplain and Marguerite Pohok, the A.F.D. for the Red Cross sent a letter to the Leominster Journal thanking those who helped with the 'Victory Tea' and also mentioning those who had contributed flowers and other items for the hospital.

There were two letters in the paper thanking the American servicemen for providing the party for the children. The one from the secretary of Leominster Branch Labour Party took the opportunity to make a dig at the council stating in his letter:

"It is strange that it should be left to the Americans to provide enjoyment for our children – something they have not enjoyed for the past six years. I think this should have been done by some of the so-called 'Leading lights' of Leominster who so readily came forward on other occasions. But perhaps it is because the masses of children came from the middle classes and they could not spare time to see our children enjoy themselves. … Until we make our Council really representative of the people who live in our Borough the great majority of whom are respectable working class citizens, so long will, I am afraid the children of Leominster be overlooked at times of National rejoicing." (Leominster Journal 25/5/45)

CHAPTER 10

A FRAGMENT OF HISTORY

By the beginning of August 1945 all of the American servicemen had left Leominster. Green Lane Camp was eventually demolished and houses were built on the site.

At Berrington Park the tents were taken down and the nissen huts were used for housing German and Italian Prisoners of War. From 1946 the buildings were occupied by 'squatters' who were awaiting permanent accommodation in the area. Some of the 'squatters' were soldiers, who had returned from the war, married and set up home there because there was nowhere else to live. In 1949 the water tower was taken down at the insistence of the second Lord Cawley who thought it was an eyesore. Also in 1949 Farmer William Edwards was offered his farmland back when it was derequisitioned. The huts were demolished in 1954. A small copse, now known as Camp Wood, was planted near North Lodge to hide most of the hostel remains. In the woodland traces can still be seen of the hut bases.

The Barons Cross site was used by the Polish Resettlement Corps after the war as Polish Hospital 340. (Oboz Rodzin Wojsk 340 Szipal Wajenny) In 1947 it was commanded by Lieutenant Colonel Stanislaw Szostak. Mr Marian Maczka spent a short time there in the period 1946–47. He had served with the Polish 458th Motorized Workshop, 2nd Corps as a cadet during the war. At the end of the war he travelled from Naples to the U.K. Once in England, Marian was assigned to a military barracks in Friar Street, Hereford. Each day he would report for orders to Foxley Camp (near Hereford), which was the Polish H.Q. He would often be sent

CHAPTER 10 – A FRAGMENT OF HISTORY

BMS

Telegraphic Address: "TRAVAUX, BIRMINGHAM."
Telephone Number: Mid. 7121 Ext. 174

Your reference ....

Our reference DLA/BM.1A/HS.23

MINISTRY OF WORKS,
GOVERNMENT BUILDINGS SOUTH, (P.8)
ASHLEY STREET,
BIRMINGHAM, 5

9th December, 1949

Dear Sir,

Ministry of Agriculture Hostel,
Berrington Park, Near Leominster

It is proposed to de-requisition the surplus land here, retaining the site of the Hostel only.

2. Before taking the necessary steps to implement this decision, I should be very glad if you would advise me whether you would be agreeable to accepting the de-requisitioning of the land shewn edged red on the attached plan, this Ministry continuing to hold the area shewn hatched green.

3. Perhaps you would be good enough to write me on the matter stating your views.

Yours faithfully,

(G. C. GAEL)
for District Estate Surveyor

W. E. Edwards, Esq.,
　Lower Ashton Farm,
　　Berrington,
　　　Near Leominster,
　　　　Herefordshire.

Letter from Ministry of Works (P. Edwards).

Marian Maczka on his bike 1947.

CHAPTER 10 – A FRAGMENT OF HISTORY

to work on farms in the local area. One day, as he was getting into the truck to take him to a farm, he slipped and broke his leg. He was first taken to the sick bay at Foxley but it wasn't equipped to deal with his injury so he was sent to Barons Cross where he spent six weeks in the camp hospital.

When he reported back to duty at Foxley, Marian was given a bicycle and put to work as an errand boy. Misfortune was to strike again when he was cycling along the narrow roads around Foxley. A truck came along on the wrong side of the road and knocked him off his bike. Marian damaged his knee and was sent back to Barons Cross for five more weeks before he could return to his duties.

In a Commons sitting in 1956 questions were asked about the use of the land at Barons Cross. Mr Baldwin requested that the land be released so that housing could be built there. The Secretary of State for War, Mr Hare, refused stating that the Ministry of Defence still needed the land. Mr Baldwin asked:

"Is my Right Hon. friend aware that this camp of 34 acres which is served with roads, sewage and light is very suitable for extending building accommodation which the local authority wants and is also an attractive site for industry? Is my Right Hon. friend aware that no matter what his information maybe to the contrary, this camp is one which is redundant in the opinion of the local people? Will he send someone down to have a local inquiry to see whether the loss of this land to the local authority by his retention of it may be avoided?" (27/11/1956 Commons)

Mr Hare's reply was:

"As I think my Hon. friend knows, this camp has a dual purpose. In peace time it is not, I admit, fully occupied, but as my Hon. friend knows, this land is required should an emergency ever arise and it is for that reason we find it difficult to adapt the suggestion my Hon. friend has made. I have not had any application for the use of this land for houses. I have had applications for its use for industrial purposes and for its use for a highway depot but there has been no application to me, apart from what my Hon. friend has just said, for this land to be used as housing." (27/11/1956 Commons)

From 1956 to 1958 the camp was used by the R.A.M.C. After the R.A.M.C. left the camp where the nurses' living quarters were, at the end of the camp, were demolished and houses were built on the land. The remainder of the site became a turkey farm.

Enlisted mens' buildings c1990 (M. Collins).

Interior of ward c1990 (M. Collins).

CHAPTER 10 – A FRAGMENT OF HISTORY

Covered walkway c1990 (M. Collins).

Water Tower c1990 (M. Collins).

Original workmens' huts used as enlisted mens' quarters c1990 (M. Collins).

View of covered walkway c1990 (M. Collins).

CHAPTER 10 – A FRAGMENT OF HISTORY

Aerial view of Barons Cross Camp c1990. Housing can be seen on the part of the site which was the nurses' quarters (David Ford).

In 2004, after the camp had been empty for several years, there was a proposal for its demolition and redevelopment of the land for housing. Taylor Woodrow proposed to build 425 properties, a community centre and play area on the site.

At this point in time Barons Cross was the country's largest surviving disused wartime hospital camp. Apart from loss of the the nurses' headquarters it was virtually intact. There were some objections to its demolition. One of the strongest came from 'The Barons Cross Camp Preservation Group', which wanted to see the retention of the former officers' mess block to use as a community centre and to provide a historical record of the site. Councillor Richard Westwood, spokesmen for the group stated:

Officers' mess building c1990 (M. Collins).

Remaining building on the Barons Cross site 2010 (M. Collins).

CHAPTER 10 – A FRAGMENT OF HISTORY

"It is vital to preserve a fragment of Britain's largest surviving Second World War military site where more than 70 wartime buildings are still standing." (Thisisherefordshire)

Taylor Woodrow felt that the officers' mess building was unsuitable for a community building because of its location, shape and poor condition and proposed that a purpose built one in a more central location would be better, but Richard Westwood argued that:

"The majority of the footprint of the H. block is not designated for housing. Saving it as a community centre would not disrupt current plans much." (Thisisherefordshire)

Sadly in 2006 the buildings, including the officers' mess, were demolished. One small building was saved from demolition because it was home to a group of badgers at the time. Unfortunately due to the economic recession the plans to build houses on the site did not materialise and the site remains empty with the one building standing and evidence of hut bases in the undergrowth. Much of the site has returned to nature and is an ideal spot for local people to walk their dogs.

APPENDIX 1

ABBREVIATIONS

A.F.D.	Assistant Field Director (Supervisor of the Red Cross at a base)
A.R.C.	American Red Cross
A.W.O.L.	Absent Without Leave
C.O.	Commanding Officer
E.E.N.T.	Eyes, Ears, Nose and Throat
E.T.O.	European Theatre of Operations
P.T.O.	Pacific Theater of Operations
H.Q.	Headquarters
K.P.	Kitchen Police (duties in the kitchen)
K.I.A.	Killed in Action
M.I.A.	Missing in Action
W.I.A.	Wounded in Action
L.S.T.	Landing Ship Tank
L.C.T.	Landing Craft Tank

APPENDIX 1 – ABBREVIATIONS

M.P.	Military Police
N.C.O.	Non-Commissioned Officer
Col.	Colonel
Cpl.	Corporal
Lt.	Lieutenant
Maj.	Major
Pfc.	Private First Class
Pvt.	Private
Sgt.	Sergeant
Tec.4.	Technician 4th Grade
O.D.	Olive Drab, referring to military colour of khaki
P.A.	Public Address system
P.O.E.	Port of Embarkation
P.O.W.	Prisoner of War
P.X.	Post Exchange – U.S. equivalent of NAAFI
R.A.F.	Royal Air Force
R.A.M.C.	Royal Army Medical Corps
R & R	Rest and Recuperation
U.S.O.	United Services Organizations
W.V.S.	Womens' Voluntary Service – British civilian voluntary organisation
Comm. Z.	Communication Zone – area behind the combat zone i.e. U.K.
Z.I.	Zone of the Interior (U.S.)

APPENDIX 2

GLOSSARY

Ambulatory – patients able to walk.

Assigned – having permanent duties at a base.

Limited Assignment – having temporary duties at a base.

Litter – stretcher.

Convalescent Hospital (C.H.) – treated convalescing troops sent from station or general hospitals.

General Hospital (G.H.) – hospital with 1082 beds (although at times when the need arose this number was larger). Mainly intended for soldiers wounded during combat.

Station Hospital (S.H.) – hospital with 834 beds serving the needs of troops in training. Often attached to a base.

Forward Echelon – troops in a combat zone.

Operation Overlord – codename for Allied invasion of France.

APPENDIX 2 – GLOSSARY

Operation Bolero – codename for the build up of troops in Britain in readiness for D-Day.

Mess hall – dining room.

Motor Pool – unit that repaired and maintained the vehicles attached to a unit.

First echelon maintenance – daily inspection, servicing, fuelling, carrying out minor repairs to vehicles.

Second echelon maintenance – preventative inspections, adjustments, carrying out repairs and replacements which can be accomplished with hand tools and mobile equipment e.g. adjusting valves, changing engines.

Replacement Depot – transit camp for personnel awaiting assignment.

Special Service – education and entertainment section responsible for the morale of troops on a base.

Western Base Section – western quarter of U.K.

APPENDIX 3

AMERICAN UNITS BASED IN LEOMINSTER, 1944–1945

The following information on the locations and units comes from U.K. Station Lists that were published at various intervals during the war. They show where U.S. Army/Army Air Force units were on a particular day. It does not mean that the unit arrived or departed on that date, only that is where it was.

A minus sign (-) indicates that part of the unit was elsewhere.

21 FEBRUARY 1944

5 Ranger Infantry Battalion, Headquarters
5 Ranger Infantry Battalion, Headquarters Company
5 Ranger Infantry Battalion, Company A
5 Ranger Infantry Battalion, Company B
5 Ranger Infantry Battalion, Company C
5 Ranger Infantry Battalion, Company D
5 Ranger Infantry Battalion, Company E
5 Ranger Infantry Battalion, Company F
5 Ranger Infantry Battalion, Medical Detachment

APPENDIX 3 – AMERICAN UNITS BASED IN LEOMINSTER, 1944–1945

12 Field Artillery Observation Battalion, Advance Detachment
33 Signal Construction Battalion, Advance Detachment
66 Ordnance Battalion, Advance Detachment
196 Field Artillery Group, Advance Detachment
312 Ordnance Battalion, Advance Detachment
314 Ordnance Battalion, Advance Detachment
316 Ordnance Battalion (-), Advance Detachment
317 Ordnance Battalion, Advance Detachment
385 Anti-Aircraft Artillery AW Battalion (Self-Propelled)
1025 Signal Company (Service Group)

31 MARCH 1944

12 Field Artillery Observation Battalion, Battery B
33 Station Hospital (-), Headquarters

30 APRIL 1944

33 Station Hospital (-), Headquarters
76 General Hospital (-), Headquarters
76 General Hospital, Medical Detachment
193 Field Artillery Group (Motorized), Headquarters
193 Field Artillery Group (Motorized), H.Q. Battery
315 Medical Battalion, Company C
315 Engineer Combat Battalion (-), Headquarters
315 Engineer Combat Battalion, H.Q. & Service Company
315 Engineer Combat Battalion, Medical Detachment
359 Infantry Regiment (-), Headquarters
359 Infantry Regiment, Headquarters Company
359 Infantry Regiment, 2 Battalion, Headquarters
359 Infantry Regiment, 2 Battalion, H.Q. Company
359 Infantry Regiment, 2 Battalion, Company E
359 Infantry Regiment, 2 Battalion, Company F

359 Infantry Regiment, 2 Battalion, Company G
359 Infantry Regiment, 2 Battalion, Company H
359 Infantry Regiment, 3 Battalion, Headquarters
359 Infantry Regiment, 3 Battalion, H.Q. Company
359 Infantry Regiment, 3 Battalion, Company I
359 Infantry Regiment, 3 Battalion, Company K
359 Infantry Regiment, 3 Battalion, Company L
359 Infantry Regiment, 3 Battalion, Company M
359 Infantry Regiment, Anti-Tank Company
359 Infantry Regiment, Cannon Company
359 Infantry Regiment, Medical Detachment
359 Infantry Regiment, Service Company

31 MAY 1944

7 Armored Division, Advance Detachment
76 General Hospital, Headquarters
315 Engineer Combat Battalion (-), Headquarters
315 Medical Battalion, Company C
359 Infantry Regiment (-), Headquarters

30 JUNE 1944

76 General Hospital (-), Headquarters (-)

31 AUGUST 1944

736 Field Artillery Battalion (8 inch How)
943 Field Artillery Battalion (155 How)
16 Field Artillery Observation Battalion
135 General Hospital
Detachment of Patients 4177 HP

APPENDIX 3 – AMERICAN UNITS BASED IN LEOMINSTER, 1944–1945

31 OCTOBER 1944

135 General Hospital
Detachment of Patients 4177 Hospital Plant

25 NOVEMBER 1944

45 Signal Construction Battalion (Heavy)
135 General Hospital
475 Collection Company
481 Collection Company
Detachment of Patients 4177 HP

16 DECEMBER 1944

24 Signal Construction Battalion (H)
45 Signal Construction Battalion (H)
135 General Hospital
475 Collection Company
481 Collection Company
3187 Signal Service Battalion
4177 Hospital Plant Detachment of Patients

2 MAY 1945

135 General Hospital
378 Military Police Patrol Detachment
Detachment of Patients 4177 Hospital Plant

APPENDIX 4

U.S. ARMY HOSPITALS IN U.K. 1944

PLANT NO.	SITE	HOSPITAL UNIT	PLANT NO.	SITE	HOSPITAL UNIT
4100	Truro	314SH	4154	Blockley	327SH
4101	Tavistock	115SH	4155	Moreton	
4102	Moretonhampstead		4156	Fairford	
4103	Newton Abbot	124GH	4157	Salisbury	152SH
4104	Exeter	36SH	4165	Tyntesfield	74GH
4105	Barnstaple	313SH	4166	Bristol	117GH
4106	Bishops Lydeard	185GH	4167	Stoneleigh	307SH
4107	Norton Manor	101GH	4168	Bromsgrove	123SH
4108	Taunton	67GH	4169	Wolverley	52GH
4109	Axminster	315SH	4170	Bewdley	297GH
4110	Yeovil, Houndstone	169GH	4171	Bewdley	114GH
4111	Yeovil, Lufton	121GH	4172	Blackmore Park	93GH
4112	Sherborne	228SH	4173	Blackmore Park	155GH
4113	Frome St Quintin	305SH	4174	Malvern Wells	96GH
4114	Blandford	22GH	4175	Malvern Wells	53GH
4115	Blandford	119GH	4176	Malvern Wells	55GH
4116	Blandford	125GH	4177	Leominster	135GH
4117	Blandford	131GH	4178	Foxley	123GH
4118	Blandford	140GH	4179	Foxley	156GH

APPENDIX 4 – U.S. ARMY HOSPITALS IN U.K. 1944

4119	Wimborne	106GH	4180	Kington	122GH
4120	Ringwood	104GH	4181	Kington	107GH
4121	Netley	110SH	4182	Abergavenny	279SH
4122	Winchester	38SH	4183	Rhyd Lafar	81GH
4123	Stockbridge	34GH	4184	Carmarthen	232SH
4124	Odstock	158GH	4185	Lichfield	33SH
4125	Grimsdith	250SH	4186	Shugborough	312SH
4126	Warminster	216GH	4187	Sudbury Derby	182GH
4127	Tidworth	3SH	4188	Whittington	68GH
4129	Perham Downs	103GH	4189	Oteley Deer Park	137GH
4129	Everleigh	187GH	4190	Overton	83GH
4130	Devizes	141GH	4191	Penley	129GH
4131	Devizes	128GH	4192	Iscoyd Park	82GH
4132	Erlestoke Park	102GH	4193	Saighton	109GH
4133	Bath	160SH	4194	Clatterbridge	157GH
4134	Falfield	94GH	4195	Stockton Heath	168SH
4135	Malmesbury	120SH	4196	Davey Hulme	10SH
4136	Lydiard Park	302SH	4197	Glasgow	316SH
4137	Swindon	154GH	4198	Harrogate	115GH
4138	Chiseldon	130SH	4199	Harrogate	116GH
4139	Marlborough	347SH	4200	Mansfield	184GH
4140	Hermitage	98GH	4201	Nocton Hall	7GH
4141	Checkendon	306GH	4202	Allington	348SH
4142	Kingwood	304GH	4203	Lilford Hall	303SH
4143	Wheatley	97GH	4204	Diddington	49SH
4144	Headington	91GH	4205	Cambridge	163GH
4145	Middleton Stanley	318SH	4206	Newport	280SH
4146	Ramsden	317SH	4207	Braintree	121SH
4147	Burford	61GH	4208	Acton, Suffolk	136SH
4148	Fairford	186GH	4209	Redgrave Park	65GH
4149	Cirencester	188GH	4210	Wymondham	231SH
4150	Cirencester	192GH	4211	North Mimms	1GH
4151	Daglinworth	111GH	4212		
4152	Stowell Park	160GH	4213	Packington	77SH
4153	Ullenwood	110GH	4261	London	16SH

ACKNOWLEDGEMENTS

In grateful acknowledgment to the following people and organisations for their stories and support in writing this book:

Colin Beard, Zosia Biegus, Rosanne and Joy Bliss, Jon Bowen, Maurice Bursey, Pauline Davies, Tim Eastman, Pam Edwards, Mrs David Finn, Derek Ford, Lt. Col. Philip Grinton, Don Hartman and the Veteran's Memorial Hall, William Healey, Christine Hood, Janice Imgrun, Roland Johnson, Westley Johnston, Bill Laws, Malcolm Mason, Marian Maczka, Ben Major, Leon Minvielle, Edward Moy, Glenn and Carol Mounts, Eileen Murray, Gene Overholt, Chad Phillips, John Phillips, Chris Sanson, Neil and Adrian Turley, Richard Westwood, Shirley Whittall, Mick Wilks, Linda Vines.

Organisations:
Herefordshire Records Office
Hereford Times
Leominster Journal
Leominster Library
Leominster Museum
76th General Hospital Military Archives and Red Cross Archives
135th General Hospital Military Archives and Red Cross Archives
WW2 U.S. Medical Research Center

BY THE SAME AUTHORS

Letters for Victory, Brewin Books, 1993.

Somewhere in the Midlands, Brewin Books, 1998.

They Also Serve, Brewin Books, 2001.

Camp Foxley, Brewin Books, 2005.

Blackmore Park in World War II, Brewin Books, 2008.

Return to Duty, Brewin Books, 2010.